SECRETS
of
Professional
Sports Betting

Dedicated to my family and friends
who are always there for me

SECRETS of Professional Sports Betting

MICHAEL KOCHAN

CARDOZA PUBLISHING

Cardoza Publishing is the foremost gaming and gambling publisher in the world with a library of almost 200 up-to-date and easy-to-read books and strategies. These authoritative works are written by the top experts in their fields and with more than 10 million books in print, represent the best-selling and most popular gaming books anywhere.

2010 PRINTING

Library of Congress Catalog No: 2008933840
ISBN 10:   1-58042-256-X
ISBN 13: 978-1-58042-256-7

Visit our new web site (www.cardozabooks.com) or write us for a full list of books, advanced and computer strategies.

CARDOZA PUBLISHING
P.O. Box 98115, Las Vegas, NV 89193
Toll Free Phone (800)577-WINS
email: cardozabooks@aol.com
www.cardozabooks.com

Table of Contents

5. 11 DO'S FOR SUCCESSFUL SPORTS HANDICAPPING 35

6. 9 DON'TS FOR SUCCESSFUL SPORTS HANDICAPPERS 61

CHAPTER

INTRODUCTION

This book is filled with tips, methods, strategies and ideas to help you win money betting on sports, not only in the four major North American sports—football, basketball, hockey and basketball—but in many other sports like boxing, tennis and the Olympics. You'll learn to profitably bet pro games as well as pre-season, college, and of course, playoffs and championship games.

You cannot pretend to be a psychic and pick winners based on hunches or feelings. You must have a legitimate reason for every bet you make. If you don't, you are just playing guessing games. That's not the path to making money at sports betting.

When you pick a game to wager on, you are not just trying to be smart and pick a winner based on a spread. You are investing your money in the players or the team. If you bet on the Red Sox and Josh Beckett on a certain day, you are investing in them. If you bet on the Lakers and Kobe Bryant to cover the spread, or if you wager on Tom Brady and the New England Patriots, you are investing your money in them, the same way you would in a stock. You are investing in them because they have been consistent in the past and, based on your research, you believe that they will come through again.

Each game can be dissected so that you can find good reasons to place a wager to defeat the Vegas spread or your sports book. You'll learn to analyze the important factors of a good bet as well as the key questions to ask. For example: Is the team good at home? Are they playing well now? Are there any serious injuries? Any serious mismatches? What was the tempo in their previous matches this year? Is the spread off base?

I am not here to teach you the ins and outs of every sport. You must learn that on your own by watching and analyzing games. But I will teach you to be selective and only place bets that you determine are favorable. That will give you the best chances for success as a sports gambler.

My book will show you how to turn sports knowledge, information and betting strategies into winning money. You still call the shots. You still have to know sports. Just think of me as a good coach who is helping you become the best sports handicapper you can be. And one who will help you make money beating the bookie!

CHAPTER
2

THE BASICS OF SPORTS BETTING

This section is designed for readers who are new to sports handicapping and are not familiar with different betting opportunities and wagering formats. If you are an experienced sports bettor, you can skip this section.

In sports gambling, you can wager on any sporting event that you are able to find a line on. Basketball, football, baseball and hockey are the four main team sports that you can wager on in North America. You can also bet on tennis, soccer, rugby, NASCAR, golf and many other sports. As a sports handicapper, any league or game about which you have knowledge is a potential wagering opportunity. Most bookmakers will allow you to bet a minimum of $5 or $10 on a given wager and a maximum in the thousands of dollars.

In this section, I will define the basics of four different types of wagers: The point spread, the money line, over/under bets, and future wagers. Point spreads are used mostly in football and basketball wagering, while money lines predominantly are used in baseball, hockey and tennis wagering. Over/unders and future wagers can be made in almost any sporting event.

THE POINT SPREAD

The point spread is designed to set a value on a given game using a points handicap. For example, suppose the Utah Jazz are at home playing the Minnesota Timberwolves. The linesmaker has set the line for Utah to be 8 1/2 point favorites, and Minnesota as 8 1/2 point underdogs. With every line, there is a favorite and an underdog. The favorite is valued by the linesmakers to be the better pick in the given match. The line is based on a value or *perceived* value of the quality of the two teams. In this example, the linesmaker sees Utah as 8 1/2 points better than Minnesota tonight. Once the line is available for wagering, people will place their bets on either Utah or Minnesota based on those assigned points.

Since the line is set on Utah as a favorite by 8 1/2 points, a wager on Utah will be a winning one if they win the game by 9 points or more. If they win by 8 points or less, or if they lose the game outright, a wager on Utah will be a losing one. You can also wager on Minnesota. Since they are 8 1/2 point underdogs, if they win the game outright or lose the game by 8 points or less, your wager is a winner. If they lose the game by 9 points or more, your wager is a loser.

The simple way to do the math at the end is to add the number of points to the underdog's score that the favorite is favored by. If the underdog ends up with more points than the other team, you win your wager. In this example with the 8 1/2 point spread, if the final score in the game is Minnesota 98 at Utah 104, then you can simply add 98 for Minnesota (underdog) with

8 1/2 points to get a total of 106 1/2 for Minnesota. Always add the points with the underdog's final total. You now get a final score in the gambling world of 106 1/2 for Minnesota to 104 for Utah. Using this method of looking at it, you can see that Minnesota is a winning wager while Utah is a losing one.

If the spread in the game makes Utah a favorite by only 5 points, and if they win the game by exactly 5 points, all bets on Utah and Minnesota are refunded and all wagers are considered a tie or a push—no one makes or loses any money.

Any point-spread wager goes hand in hand with a simple money line. The standard is -110, but can vary depending on the sports book, game and type of wager. This means that with point-spread wagers, for every $110 that you wager, you will win $100. The -110 can be broken down as well. A $55 dollar wager profits $50; an $11 wager profits $10; and a $1,100 wager profits $1,000.

You might be wondering why you don't win $110 when you bet $110. Where does the extra money go? The extra money goes to the bookmaker as his commission for taking wagers on games. If the bookmaker is able to balance his books and receive equal betting in a given game, then he will be happy to collect his commission or *vigorish*. Bookmakers do not always balance the books, but in the long run, they are able to make money because, with all point-spread wagers, they always pay less in return than they accept as risk in a given match. With the thousands, if not millions, of wagers they take, that advantage ensures them financial stability.

THE MONEY LINE

Most games have wagering available with no point spread, just a strict money line on the game. These wagers are simple to understand. With a money line, your team just has to win the game for you to win your wager. They do not have to win by a certain amount of points. If your team wins by 1 point or 20 points, you still win your wager. Or if they lose by 1 point or 20 points, you will lose your wager.

Money line odds are easy to calculate. Just put a decimal point to the left of the last two zeros in the odds. With a favorite, divide the amount you want to wager by the odds. With an underdog, multiply your wager amount by the odds. It's very simple. Let's say the Utah Jazz are the favorite at -350 with the Minnesota Timberwolves the underdog at +310. To calculate net returns with Utah, you convert the -350 into 3.50. If you want to wager $1,000 you take 1,000 (amount wagered) divided by 3.50 (odds), which equals 285.71. This means that if you wager $1,000 on Utah at -350 and they win the game, you will profit by $285.71.

On the other hand, if you wager $1,000 on Minnesota and they win the game, you will profit $3,100. Convert the +310 into 3.10. In this case 1,000 (amount wagered) multiplied by 3.1 (odds) equals $3,100 for Minnesota. The only money line wagers that would involve a push would be in a league that actually has ties. If your game ends in a tie, no money is won and no money is lost. As you can see, the bookmaker's profit margin is the vigorish/commission, the difference between the -310 and the +350 with the bets he accepts.

Remember that with money line wagers, there is no point spread. You risk more money to win less money on the favorite, and with the underdog your return on a winning wager is more than the amount you risk.

You'll find a section dedicated to money-line wagering opportunities in a later chapter.

OVER/UNDER WAGERS

Over/under wagers are not based on which team wins the game. They are based on how many points or runs or goals are attained in a given sporting match. Over/under spreads come with a total number, and are accompanied with the standard -110 money line. For example, going back to the example game between the Minnesota Timberwolves and the Utah Jazz, a linesmaker may set the line at 189 points. If you think the total number of points scored in the game will be over 189 points, you can place an "over" wager. If you think the total amount of points scored in the game will be under 189 points, you can place an "under" wager. If the total points scored in the game is over 189, the over will be a winning wager, while any total under 189 will make the under a winning wager. If exactly 189 points are scored, all wagers are a push and no money is won or lost by bettors.

Suppose the final score in the game is Minnesota 98 at Utah 104, a total of 202 points. Since 202 went over the total spread of 189, any over wagers made on this game are winners, and any under wagers are losers. Since over/under wagers are accompanied with the -110 money line, if you wagered $220 on the over, your profit would be $200. If you wagered $220 on the under, your bet is a loser and you would lose $220. Later in this book, you will find advice on various over/under strategies.

FUTURE WAGERS

Future wagers are bets that are based on a future outcome in a sporting league. Who will win the championship? Who will win the conference? Who will win the division? Who will win MVP? There are some examples of future bets; there are many more. A future wager can involve almost any kind of future result. Futures usually involve many teams in one wager, while regular bets involve just two teams. Future wagers are paid at a later date, while regular game wagers can be settled the same day the game is finished

Let's use the NFL for an example. Most bookmakers offer odds on who will win the Super Bowl. Like some future lines, this line is available all season, though the odds will forever be changing based on the success and failure of different teams at various points in the season.

Here is a hypothetical list that a bookmaker may give you of the odds that a football team will win the Super Bowl.

New England	+300	New York Jets	+2500
Indianapolis	+900	Carolina	+1900
Pittsburgh	+1200	Baltimore	+6500
New York Giants	+900	Houston	+5000
San Diego	+1200	Washington	+4000
Denver	+1500	St. Louis	+3000
Green Bay	+900	Tennessee	+1600
Dallas	+750	Cleveland	+1700
New Orleans	+950	Tampa Bay	+2000
Jacksonville	+1100	Detroit	+4500
Chicago	+1600	Buffalo	+3000
Kansas City	+5000	Arizona	+3000
Seattle	+2000	Oakland	+4000
Atlanta	+3500	Philadelphia	+3000
San Francisco	+4000	Cincinnati	+2200
Miami	+15000	Minnesota	+2000

You can wager on any one of these teams. If your team ends up winning the Super Bowl, your wager is a winner. If your team doesn't win the Super Bowl, your wager is a loser. The odds are very simple. It may confuse you to see all those zeros, but their meaning is easy to understand: They tell you how much you will win if you bet $100. For example if you wager $100 on Dallas to win the Super Bowl, then you will win $750 if they win it. If they don't win the Super Bowl, you lose the $100. If Dallas wins the Super Bowl, all other NFL Super Bowl future wagers will be considered a loser that season.

With all future wagers, you always get back your original stake in addition to your winnings if your bet ends up winning. For example, in November you bet on Dallas to win the Super Bowl. The odds you receive are the odds that you get at the time you place your wager, and they remain the same until the end. You're right: Dallas wins it. You profit $750 and get back your $100 wager for a gross return of $850, which can warm your hands considerably on a cold day in February.

If the odds still seem complex, use the same method you would use on any money line wager. Let's say that you bet Minnesota at +2000. Put a decimal point to the left of the last two numerals, so that it becomes 20.00. Now multiply the 20.00 by any amount you want to wager on Minnesota. If you want to wager $25, multiply 25 (your wagering amount) by 20.00 (your odds). If Minnesota wins the Super Bowl this NFL season, $500 will be your profit. You can do this with all money line wagers.

Some bookmakers list their odds in fractions for some wagers. In that case, use your basic math skills to turn that fraction into a real number. For example, 12/5 odds is the same thing as +240; or 3/2 odds is the same thing as +150. To calculate your odds, just take the first number and divide it by the second number. Using 3/2 as an example, 3 divided by 2 is 1.5. Therefore, 1.5 odds or +150 are your odds. You can multiply the 1.5 by the amount you want to wager to see what your profit will be on a winning wager.

Be sure that you have a good grasp of the basic information in this section before implementing the tips and strategies in this book. Once you have a few wagers under your belt, the mathematics of everything will become simple to follow. Now, here are three basic yet pivotal tips for novice sports bettors.

CHAPTER
3

3 TOP TIPS FOR NOVICE SPORTS BETTORS

1. SET YOUR GOAL TO MAKE MONEY

The first rule of sports gambling: Establish making money as your gambling goal. Making money should be your only goal in sports wagering—everything else is secondary. If you gamble just to have fun, you will lose. If you gamble for a hobby, you will lose. If you're gambling to spice up your life with some action, ditto: You will lose. Go to a concert, play a sport, go to a bar, or go dancing—whatever you do for recreation. But leave gambling out off that list.

Don't adopt the attitude that you will "budget" $150 a week for your gambling. You will not be dealing with budgets. Budgets are for people who spend money. Think of your money in terms of a bankroll that you want to grow over time rather than spend over a weekend.

Think long-term. Wager to make money over the long haul, keeping in mind that your goal in gambling is to consistently make a profit. The only real emotion you should feel is overwhelming pride when you show a net profit at the end of the year.

2. KEEP YOUR EMOTIONS IN CHECK

The less emotion you invest in your sports gambling, the more successful you will become as a bettor. You might be wondering, "How could you be wagering on sports without feeling any rush or emotion?" You will usually have feelings about the action in the game, but the key to success is to not allow your emotions to influence your wagers. You must manage your emotions.

Everybody who starts gambling feels the rush of emotions, up and down like a roller coaster. As a very young man, I remember once making a $2 sports lottery wager and watching the games on TV. I got a sincere rush from that little bet that I made. Every person in this world feels things to a different degree, but no matter what level of emotion you feel, you must control it.

The only care you should have is what's happening with your money. The absence of emotion attached to your wagers will help you choose your bets with your head instead of your heart.

3. DON'T GAMBLE FOR THE ACTION ALONE

Action is the term used by gamblers when they are in on a bet. Action also refers to the rush that they feel during the bet. However, action is what gets people addicted to gambling; it is just a temporary feeling or high that fades when the game is over. If you always think long-term, you will not force bets for the sake of action.

The key to success is having a logical reason to make a bet before you place each wager. Your logic must override your desire for action. Don't make a bet on Monday Night Football because the game is on TV and you want action on it. I know that this temptation is hard to resist. Wager on that game because you think you have a solid bet to make.

When I first started gambling, I felt a great rush in watching games that I bet on or following the scoreboard on TV or radio. I now like to think of that emotion as an artificial rush. Indeed, after placing thousands of bets over the years, the rush has subsided considerably. These days, I easily control the bets I make with my head rather than my heart.

You might find it very stressful to watch a game that you have a lot of money riding on. The key to reducing your stress is remembering that once you have placed your bet and the game has started, you cannot control the outcome of the game (although you may be able to hedge your bet at halftime). So, try to remain calm during games, win or lose. And definitely refrain from forcing bets just to get in on the action.

Some of the best days I've ever had gambling were days when I made no bets at all, days when I would have lost money because I had been thinking of making suspect bets. As in sports, sometimes a good call is no call at all.

In addition to self-control, money management is crucial to your success as a sports handicapper. Managing your funds requires savvy and discipline. Here are seven of my top tips to help you manage your bankroll.

CHAPTER 4

7 IMPORTANT MONEY MANAGEMENT TIPS

1. BET BIGGER ON YOUR MOST SECURE WAGERS

Success in sports gambling is dependant not only on the quality of the picks you make and the self control you exercise, but just as importantly, the management of your bankroll. To make a profit each year, I suggest using this simple approach: Regardless of money line odds and spreads, put your big money bets on the wagers you believe are your most secure, and put small money bets on the wagers that you believe give you only a small advantage.

Before making each wager, roughly calculate what percentage chance you think you have of winning. You might believe that some bets have a 50 to 59 percent chance of winning, others a 60 to 65 percent chance, some a 65 to 80 percent chance. You may even find a very few that you think have an 80 percent or better chance of winning. You may be wondering what an 80 percent or better wager could be. I found one during the 2007 NFL season: I was able to wager on Tom Brady after Week 8 to win the NFL MVP at even odds. I knew that, barring injury, the award was his.

However, do not wager higher amounts because you might be running hot or cold. The hot-and-cold method will kill you! You will end up forcing big money wagers on poor quality games, and wagering less money on good games or picks! Don't believe in "hot or cold." Believe in finding high-percentage wagers and fluctuating the amounts of your bet according to the strength of each bet. This is the best way to ensure long-term profit. Betting the same amount of money on every pick you make is an unsuccessful approach in wagering. You need to capitalize financially on your best picks.

You may have read that all you have to do is win 53 percent or higher of your bets to show a profit in the long run. That way of thinking will not make you money! Which way of thinking will make money? Here it is again: The more secure a bet you have, the more you wager. One of your goals should be to win at least 66 percent of the big bets you make, striving for 75 percent. Of course, you will not win at that rate, but by concentrating your wagers on games with a high level of confidence and betting more on your very best games, you will increase your chances of being a profitable bettor. Note that a big bet is one that is a lot larger than your average bet. Place your big bets only when you believe they have a *very high* probability of winning.

Here is the betting plan I suggest:

Good Bet	1 Unit
Very Solid	2 Units
Great Bet	3 Units
Very Best Bet	4 Units

If you follow this big-bet plan and hover around a 50 percent winning percentage with your smaller money bets, and win at a higher percentage with your bigger bets, you will be ahead.

2. WAGER PROPORTIONATELY WITH YOUR BANKROLL

As a sports gambler, the main advantage you have over the house is that you control which games you want to bet on and how much you bet on them. These are the two keys to your success in the long run.

Another important point is this: Never fall in love with a bet to the extent that you risk almost all of your bankroll on it. I do believe in betting a lot more than your regular wager if you have a great bet, but don't bet your whole bankroll. Bet expecting to win, but leave enough margin for error so that if disaster strikes, you will survive and still remain in the sports betting business. You do this by staying within the 1 to 4 units range for your best bets.

You have to know the difference between a great bet and a good bet to determine when to bet bigger, and you need to fluctuate the amount of your bets in order to maximize your profits. When you wager the maximum bet, it should be one that you have the maximum confidence in. This might be a money line wager of -350; or betting against an injured team; or a team resting all of its starters at a good spread; or maybe a prop or award that looks really good. In these types of situations, you should go with your maximum bet.

If your big bet loses, you can survive and live to wager another day. The crazy or the impossible happens more often than you think. I have seen Number 15 seeds beat Number 2 seeds in the NCAA tournament. I have seen the Lakers down by 27 points entering the fourth quarter come back and win a game. I've even seen John Starks dunk over Michael Jordan. And I've seen 30-point underdogs in college football win a game outright. In most pro sports and often in collegiate sports, the talent is balanced enough that things don't always go the way they are supposed to in a given game. Big upsets happen! So, never bet your whole bankroll on one wager, or even a substantial percentage of it.

In addition to regular games, I often look to make significant wagers in a best-of-seven series. Usually the better team or the team with the better match-up will win. I like to bet big in games involving injured players and shorthanded teams, and I also look for opportunities to make big wagers when a totally inappropriate spread is offered at the time I place my wager.

MVP, other award bets, and division winners are examples of long-term future bets that are other ways of making solid money in sports gambling. I like these wagers because there is more room for error. You can lose a heartbreaking game here and there along the way, yet still be in position to win if you have done your research well and picked a good team or player.

If you have found that you absolutely love a bet and want to make a large wager on it, there are a few things you should do before you place your wager. First, make a chart with two columns, one with all the positive aspects of the wager and the other with the negative points. If you have trouble thinking of any negative points, you can go on to the next step. After noting why you will win your bet, write some points from the other side of the coin as if you were going to bet the other way. I am sure you will come up with a few. If you do not come up with any logical reasons to wager the other way, speak with one or two savvy, sports-minded friends who might be able to give you another vantage point. If your friends do not have a different opinion, and they agree with you, that could be a good sign. If they give you a different way to look at your proposed bet, take their advice into account. Don't let it sway you completely, just factor in their advice.

After looking at things from all angles, if you still love your bet, then make your big wager in confidence. I know I have a great wager on my hands when I honestly believe that I will be in shock if I lose the bet. I don't find amazing wagers on a daily basis, but when I do—and when I feel this way about a wager—my bet generally destroys the spread.

3. BET IN TERMS OF UNITS

As a sports gambler, you must bet on games in proportion to your bankroll. You will be deciding how much you wager in terms of units. Let's say that $40 is the lowest average bet you would probably wager on a game. In this example then, $40 will be your assigned unit. If your lowest wager will be $20, then $20 is your unit amount.

The key with betting in units is to work with a unit number that you are comfortable with. The unit is pretty much the average lowest amount of money you would put on an individual game. With each pick you make, think in terms of units and how much do you like the pick. My approach is to make bets based on the quality of the wager, not whether I am up or down on recent wagers. The more you risk on a given wager, the more you believe it is secure.

In summary, it will be difficult to win in the long run by wagering every day or betting the same amount on each game. You should be looking every day, but many days you should pass. You must be selective and only place wagers when you have good bets. For most serious sports bettors, this might be about three to nine times a week. For others, it may be less. Remember that you are looking for an edge with your wagers—not just to have action—especially with your big bets.

4. SET FINANCIAL GOALS

A big part of money management is setting realistic financial goals. I think that setting a fixed financial goal as a sports handicapper is often setting yourself up for failure. Your goal should be to take advantage of every good and great wager that you find, and to wager more money on the better wagers. If you do this, and are a successful sports bettor, your long-term goal will usually take care of itself.

If your goal is to make $10,000 in one year, that's fine, but don't try to force wagers in order to reach your goal for the year. If you do, you will find that you are betting on games that you don't like so much, and you will end up farther away from your yearly goal as you take losses on mediocre wagers.

Don't have crazy dreams of turning a $10,000 bankroll into $70,000 in one year. That is not realistic: Your bankroll could vanish quickly if you chase the dream too hard. If you have a $10,000 bankroll for your sports handicapping and you are able to turn it into $13,000 in one year, that's not bad. Advancing to $15,000 would be very good, and doubling to $20,000 would be amazing. Even if at the end of the year, you turned your bankroll into $11,000 for a 10 percent return, that is still okay, as you are ahead of most of the public that loses money. Even if you only pulled even after all your time and hard work, that's okay as well. The experience you gained can help you show a profit the following year.

When betting units, do not suddenly increase or decrease the amount you are wagering because you're running either hot or cold. If you are hot, stick to your unit play with quality bets. Don't think that because you are up, you're playing with "their" money. No, you are always playing with *your* money, money that you have worked hard to earn. If you start betting higher amounts when you are up, eventually you will hit a cold streak. You don't want to throw away profits because of poor money management.

As your bankroll grows and you begin to enjoy some success, you might decide to increase your unit amount. A reasonable increase may be from $50 to $65, for example, or from $300 to $400. Making quality bets over a quantity of bets is the key.

5. CASH OUT ON A REGULAR BASIS

Managing your sports book accounts is important in sports wagering. I suggest cashing out of your accounts on a regular basis to help manage your money. Although you are winning, the money is not in your hands yet; it is sitting somewhere in Costa Rica, Jamaica, or England or wherever your sports book may be. The money is only really in your hands when you cash it out of your account.

A big mistake that some bettors make is betting big on a terrific wager, winning, and then using their winnings to make mediocre bets. You can lose all your profits on average wagers. If you find that you sometimes have problems making too many wagers, and you often risk money just for the sake of making a bet, a key way to control yourself is to cash out of your accounts regularly or flush out the weaker bets and play only your very strongest ones.

Plan your cash-outs around your sports betting seasons and sports wagering patterns. Keep in mind that, as a sports gambler, you must exercise solid reasoning with every bet you make; that is you must believe that you have value or advantage with every bet you place. The profits you have in your account should always be used for good or great wagers. Your profit is not money to be "played with"; it is money to be used for the next set of smart wagers. The money in your account is *your* money, not the "house's" money.

6. DO NOT GAMBLE OVER YOUR HEAD

Sports gambling can be a successful long-term venture. However, there may be times when you have taken a few big financial hits, when some of your well-researched picks are going against you. This is a time when you have to be smart and think straight rather than a time when you risk your entire sports gambling bankroll to try to recoup what you have recently lost.

You must not let your sports wagering affect your personal and professional life. Do not let your family get affected by your temporary financial loss. Do not tap into funds that were not figured into your sports gambling bankroll. If they were budgeted for something else, those funds should be used for that something else.

I also recommend that you not keep your entire bankroll in your sports book accounts at all times. However, keep a steady amount of money in your account so that you have enough liquidity to make the bets you need to make.

If you have hit a rough patch, this is a time where you must look back at your losing wagers, your mistakes, and try to figure out why they happened. One of two things may have occurred:

Looking back at these wagers, they were good or great wagers based on the information, reasoning and the statistics you used to determine these picks, but due to some unlucky circumstances in some games, you lost these bets.

Looking back at these wagers, you realize that they were not as good or great picks as you thought they were at the time. You did your analysis, but it was a little misguided. You did not take into account other key factors.

If the answer is number one, don't worry about your losing patch. You will eventually break out of it if you continue to research and think through the bets you are making. If the answer is number two, you might have to change your style or strategy with the wagers you select. Maybe you are betting too much with your heart instead of your head. At this point, you might want to lower the amount of wagers you are making and focus on making every single bet count. Self control, both emotionally and financially, will be a key to your success.

7. DO NOT LOAN MONEY TO OTHERS

Always remember the value of a dollar. And understand that that value is one thing that your friends may not realize. Do not loan money to anyone to wager on sports, even your friends. The main reason I do not believe in lending money, or even borrowing money to wager on sports is that, in the long term, borrowing is not financially responsible.

If you are to be a successful sports gambler, or at least a gambler who stays about even, then you need to maintain a bankroll with which to wager. Why would someone have to borrow money in order to make wagers? It is most likely because he has lost money recently. This person probably has already racked up a bunch of debt gambling. Someone who is in that position will probably lose again and sink into a bigger hole, and most likely will be too busy chasing losses to catch up. Advise your friend to save some money until he can get a decent bankroll together and wager on his own. And if you believe that he has a major addiction, help him quit. Loaning money can often be like giving drugs to a drug addict. Do not run up a tab with any of your friends at any time with gambling money!

It works both ways. Do not borrow money from people to wager on sports. If you are doing this, you are not a successful sports gambler and should not be putting yourself into possibly further debt. Review your style of wagering and change it to become more successful. Also, and this is important, reduce the amount of money you are betting.

Now that you understand the basics of money management and its relationship to discipline, let's move on to some good advice about how, where, why and what to wager.

CHAPTER 5

11 DO'S FOR SUCCESSFUL SPORTS HANDICAPPING

1. WAGER WITH A SPORTS BOOK

The sports gambling industry is a billion-dollar business. Currently, part of the industry operates through legal channels, while part of it runs through illegal channels. Betting on sports on a cash basis (besides provincial or state legislated sports gaming) is not legal in North America except in Las Vegas. Therefore, a lot of underground revenue in the sports gambling world exists with local bookmakers. However, over the past twenty years there has been a major rise in sports gambling through offshore sports books. These sports books operate internationally in many countries around the world.

The main advantages of betting with a sports book, is that you generally don't have to worry about getting paid. Further, you have less chance of running up major debt because you must deposit money to your sports book account before wagering, whereas with a bookie, you can place bets and pay or collect money later, which increases the financial risk. Of course, you should not be betting with money you do not currently have.

Betting with a sports book gives you a wider variety of lines to choose from. The more lines you have to choose from, the better chance you have of finding bets that are to your advantage. Good sports books offer lines in almost every major sport from football to tennis to European soccer, and some even offer lines on political events. When betting with a bookie, he might not be around when you want to place a bet and may not give you a line on an event that you want to wager on, giving you less control of your gambling potential.

With an online sports book, you will have a better record of all your bets on your computer. I suggest selecting a sports book, if you don't have one already, by searching sportsbookreview. com, one of the best sources for a sports book's reputation. Also check out osga.com for more information on sports books. The most important features of sports books are their reputation for being able to pay on time every time, the variety of lines they give, the look and ease in using their site, and their quality of customer service. The top sports books act professionally when you call them and they are ready to send you a check any time you wish to cash out.

You can wager by computer or by phone. Preferably, you should do your wagering by computer, as it keeps things simpler and gives you more control over making your selections. I almost always make my wagers by computer. The only times I don't wager online is when I am away from home. All the good sports books have 1-800 toll free numbers and many are open 24/7.

Once you are comfortable betting online with your sports book, look to open at least two other sports book accounts. Why? It's simple: You are always looking for the best line possible. Suppose you like the Seattle Sonics/Milwaukee Bucks game to go over 191 ½. Then you go to another book of yours and find the bet at 190; now you've put yourself in a better position. Don't close a sports book account, even if you are not using it for a while, because you never know when you may find a good line on a game or odd event that you can capitalize on.

Sports books give you so many different options and easy access, that sports gambling can become a hassle-free, simple and successful part of your life. They are the way to go for sports betting. Even if you live in Las Vegas where sports gambling is legal at the casinos, I still recommend doing most of your gambling online. Why would you want to drive to the nearest casino every time you find a good wager?

2. UNDERSTAND A WIDE VARIETY OF BETS

As a sports gambler you will not only be betting on individual games to make money, but on various proposition bets. The more variety available to you, the better it is. However, never allow the wide selection of picks to overwhelm you. Each pick you make should stand out for you as a good bet. If it does not stand out, you should not be wagering on it. If you know sports well, watch enough games, and follow what is going on, good or great bets will immediately become apparent to you. Stick to those opportunities.

Make sure your sports book gives you a wide variety of picks to make. Try not to worry about when you will get paid if you find a great future wager. When you can find a great pick, the potential profit is worth waiting for. Here is a partial list of wagers

(and examples) that you will be able to make. Later on I discuss
types of selections in greater detail.

Team versus the spread	(Denver Nuggets +10 points versus Indiana)
Team versus the money line	(Chicago Bulls -130 against Orlando)
Game Over/Under	(New Orleans and Boston over 186)
Individual Team Total	(New York Giants under 20 1/2 points)
Half time bets	(Minnesota -5 points 2nd half versus Utah)
Who will win the championship?	(Tampa Bay Buccaneers at 10 to 1)
Players single game stats over/under	(Tim Duncan over 23 1/2 points)
Who will win the division?	(Montreal Canadians at 4 to 1)
Team season over/under wins	(Texas over 74 1/2 wins out of 162 games)
Who will win the conference?	(New Jersey Devils at 3 to 1)
Who will win the MVP or other award?	(Yao Ming at 1 to 1 to win Rookie of the Year)
Other fantasy propositions	(Shaquille O'Neal to get more points, rebounds and blocks than points scored in Monday Night Football game)

Any type of bet in which you believe you have an advantage
is a good bet. Some of the best bets I've ever made sounded
weird, such as an NFL receiver +2 1/2 catches to a college
player's assists. The regular bets of Dallas at home -5 against

the Houston Rockets cannot be broken down enough to find an edge, but special prop bets can be, and often, great ones will be available.

3. USE THE INTERNET TO FIND AND MAKE SOLID BETS

The Internet is one of the most important tools you will need to be a successful sports gambler. Having access to it is a must. A reliable Internet service will allow you to do your research on games, exercise proper timing by obtaining the best spread possible, and follow your wagers.

When I first started wagering back in 1995, the Internet was far from being the resource that millions of people have today. At that time, I would just look at a spread and pick a winner. I had little success making money sports gambling, primarily because I had little information on which to base my picks. Today, the Internet provides up-to-the-minute information. There are many good sports websites that will give you detailed information. For example, covers.com is an excellent site for injury reports. Their injury info is up-to-date and reliable. CBS Sportsline is a good site to use to track live scores, and check standings, box scores and recaps of all major sports.

Use the sites that give you the most reliable information. A lot of the sites are geared to sports gamblers and fantasy league owners, so take advantage of them.

The information you find must be simplified to be useful in making your bets. That is, something as simple as a team's road record can help you decide on making your wager. Any information that is too complex or lists of meaningless stats will not make you money at sports gambling.

Let's analyze a statistic such as "The Miami Heat are 13 and 6 against the spread against Western Conference teams coming off of a home win." This statistic is meaningless because there is too much information to analyze. It is just a number that has been conjured up. Instead of stats like these, look for the following types of key information.

- Team records
- Team home and road records
- Injuries. Who is playing? Who is not?
- Is this team hot? Is the other team cold? How have they played recently?
- Does this player score well against defensive teams?
- Is there some public bias or Las Vegas bias with the spread?
- Is the spread off, based on the research gathered?
- Is the game played indoors?
- What is the weather going to be for this game?
- Based on the stats and on past award winners, is the player a lock to win an award?
- What was the result the last time these two teams played this season?
- Is this team consistent or unreliable?
- Who is this team's competition to win the championship or division?
- What was this team's schedule like recently?
- What are these two teams' style of play?
- How many points does this team score per game?
- How many points does this team give up per game?
- How has this team played in its last five games?

The key to success with the information you collect over the Internet is distinguishing what is relevant and what is not. The information that you will use must be real, live info. For example, real, live info is that the Detroit Pistons have won seven games in a row heading into tonight's game. This info is meaningful because you know that Detroit is a hot team and it is tough to find a reason to bet against a hot team.

A stat that is meaningless and dead is that the Detroit Pistons are 27- 13 against the Toronto Raptors. The reason that this stat is meaningless is because it's based on teams of previous years. Those teams had different players, players who may be old and grey, and are either retired or are playing on a different team. I don't know why, but in their game previews, TV announcers and newspaper columnists like to mention that, "Team A is 12-6 in their last 18 meetings against Team B." This info is almost totally meaningless in the sports gambling world. You should not place a bet based on this stat, because they're talking about previous games with previous rosters. However, if a team has won its last five matches in the NBA against an upcoming opponent, that statistic *does* have meaning. Maybe Team A cannot match-up with Team B's big frontcourt, or maybe it is some other matchup.

Having a satellite or cable sports package is a big bonus, because you can confirm information you get on the Internet in the pregame show. For example, many players will be listed as questionable, or a game-time decision for the day's game has not been verified, so you cannot be sure whether they are playing. If a game you want to wager on is starting at 8:10 p.m., you can watch the pregame show at 7:30 p.m. and the announcers will tell you for sure whether or not a player is playing. If he is playing, he will be in uniform; if he's injured and cannot play, he will be dressed in street clothes. You can get this info probably no later than 15 minutes before game time, and have enough time to make your wager by 8:00 pm.

Based on whether or not your key man is in the game, you may bet for or against that team. Or maybe you will decide to just bet that team's total under for the first half. In either case, this late information will give you the best winning possibility with the spread.

Radio and newspapers are also a good source of information, but their info is not always live. Pregame shows and the Internet give you more up-to-date info than any other source that you have access to. The key is gathering important information. In time, it will not be hard for you to distinguish key information from empty statistics. If you try to dig too deep, there probably is no worthy wager to be placed. When I find a bet that I like, a lot of my research is aimed at deciding how much I like it. The more I like it, the more I bet on it.

The average gambler spends 10 to 15 minutes analyzing a bet and two and a half hours cheering his bet on to a hopeful victory. Don't be the average gambler! Put more time into analyzing your wager than watching your wager. You should be watching games primarily to learn about teams and possible future bets. Remember that you are only in control of your bet before the games starts. Once you make the bet, your work is done. It is now the job of the athletes to help you make money by stepping up and playing the game out as you predicted.

My greatest feeling of satisfaction as a sports handicapper comes when I am able to find a great bet. Finding great bets and making winning bets is what I really enjoy—this is the challenge!

4. KNOW YOUR SPORT

Knowledge is the most important tool of a great sports handicapper. You cannot understand a sport in depth just by checking out the box scores or rosters. The more games you watch, the more you can learn about different teams. You may discover that some teams are erratic while other teams are smart and consistent.

There is no substitute for watching the teams you're wagering on play some games before you pony up your bet. For example, in March of 2008, in the NCAA basketball tournament, I made a prop wager for Tennessee, a 2-seed, to make it to the sweet 16. I made this wager based on the team's season results, and the lack of quality opponents in the first two rounds. I also got a good money line. Tennessee barely beat their 15-seeded opponent in the first round, and barely survived in overtime during their next game against Butler, not a very talented team. After watching these two games, I realized that I had won a lucky wager because Tennessee had been overrated. Tennessee had some good talent, but it was an erratic team that took crazy shots and made careless turnovers. Further, they did not play with a real point guard.

I then bet against them in their next game, against Louisville, a strong opponent and a well-coached Rick Pitino team. Louisville crushed their first two opponents in the tournament by an average margin of 24 points per game, and I had watched those two games as well. I thought that I would be in shock if Tennessee were to beat Louisville in the next round. I wagered solid money on Louisville, and with their sound fundamentals, great team defense, and overall strong team play, Louisville crushed Tennessee 79-60, destroying the 2-point spread they were favored by. I would not have learned everything about these two teams by reading a box score.

Watching teams play gives you confidence to either bet on them or bet against them.

You must also know the different variables going into a game. You have to know the leagues and the flow of their games. You have to realize that in football, the losing team will be passing a lot more than they will be running; and in college basketball, teams that love to press will inflate the scores of their games. In other words, you have to know the little things.

If you understand sports intimately, try to increase your knowledge by learning a sport that is not often wagered on. Two other sports that can be great to bet on are tennis and boxing. Sometimes you can take advantage in these situations because in low-key sports, the linemakers don't often know where to set the line.

Of course, the most high-profile major team sports are football, baseball, basketball and hockey. You cannot judge a team on paper except for baseball, to a certain degree. In baseball, each at-bat is an individual player by himself against the opposing pitcher, while in hockey, basketball and football, there is much more team play and team chemistry to consider.

A perfect example of analyzing talent versus team cohesion occurred in the 2002-2003 NBA season. The Los Angeles Clippers had a decent season the year before, winning 39 games. In the 2002-2003 season, everyone thought they would bust out and make the playoffs because they had acquired more talent. Along with the addition of point guard Andre Miller, they had great talent in Lamar Odom, Michael Olowokandi, Elton Brand and Corey Maggette. However, one thing about basketball is that there is only one ball to go around, and if each player is worrying about scoring, nobody is doing the intangibles like setting screens, rebounding and helping out on defense. The Clippers, who on paper had more talent than the previous year, struggled miserably. Players could not gel together and they finished the 2002-2003 season 27-55.

Take the other Southern California team. The Los Angeles Lakers won three championships while having only two legitimate scorers on their team, superstars Kobe Bryant and Shaquille O'Neal. In only one of the three championship seasons, they had a legitimate third scorer in Glen Rice. The Lakers played well because everyone knew who to pass the ball to and their role players fed off the stars.

My main point is that the role player is very important in team sports. If a player does the job the coach asks him to do, and does not try to do what is beyond his capability—and if everyone does what the coach asks in terms of roles—you cannot underestimate that team or bet against that team just because the players don't look that talented on paper. When analyzing a team, it is often important to analyze their substance and style of play rather than their individual talent. Some talented basketball teams take long stupid jumpers and don't move to get open, while teams like the Utah Jazz in the 1990s won games with precision cutting, passing and teamwork while having only two name players in John Stockton and Karl Malone.

When betting, stick to things you know. If you do not know college basketball, then do not bet on college basketball until you have researched enough and have watched enough games to obtain great knowledge in the sport. If you do not have the time to learn college basketball, do not bet on it. Focus on what you do know and you will have the best chance of being successful.

In addition to watching games and finding info among many sources each day, I recommend that sports bettors watch a 30-minute or one-hour recap show of the night's games on TV. Pick a quality show with a good sports ticker as well. Recap shows will help you keep up to date with the world of sports, and give you a foundation of knowledge to build upon.

5. UNDERSTAND THE PURPOSE OF THE LINE

One very important thing to remember as a sports gambler is that the line set for an individual game is made to attract an even amount of wagering on both sides. It is designed to *balance* the wagering, not a true line of value that equates the quality of each team. Bookmakers want to put themselves in a position where they can profit regardless of the result of the game.

For example, suppose the Detroit Lions are facing the Minnesota Vikings, and Minnesota is favored by 5 1/2 points. If the bookmakers can put themselves in a position where they have received $20,000 in wagers on Minnesota and $20,000 in wagers on Detroit, they will profit regardless of who wins the game. They will collect $20,000 on the losing picks and they will pay out $18,181.82 on the winning ones. Their total profit will be $1,818.18 just for collecting the bets. Although they often find that the betting public is favoring one team over another, they will move the line in the other direction when this happens to attract betting the other way to try to balance their books. Overall, the public likes betting on favorites, so with every upset that occurs in a straight-up game, the bookmakers will profit more times than not.

How do you use this information? It's easy. Often the line that comes out on a game is not set properly to reflect current information such as trades, injuries and whether a team is hot or not. When something such as an injury or trade is reported, the line may go off the board for a few hours, but it usually returns. Sometimes the line is set based on past results, but when a team changes over the season, you can take advantage of a weak line. Often, very popular teams are favored too much, creating value on the underdogs.

In the 2003 NBA season, a matchup occurred between the Minnesota Timberwolves and the Boston Celtics. Both teams were hot coming in, Minnesota having won five of their last six games and four in a row on the road, while Boston had won five in a row overall. The line was set at Boston -2 points at home. The same day, a trade was announced about three hours before tip-off. Boston traded their first three players off the bench (their sixth, seventh and eighth men) to Cleveland—almost their whole bench. There was no time for Boston to get the players that they had acquired in the trade to play, so Boston played shorthanded. Boston also lost Eric Williams, one of their team leaders, in the trade. Further, Boston's star player, Paul Pierce, was playing hurt with a calf injury.

The line in the game started to move the other way. It moved a point every half an hour or so, because the bookmakers wanted to balance their books as people started wagering on Minnesota. Before the game started, the line ended up with Minnesota at -2 points. In the big scheme of things, 2 points in a basketball game over 48 minutes is nothing, only one bucket. Realistically, the line should have moved to Minnesota by 5 or 6 points immediately after the trade was reported. Anybody who was on top of the info could have taken advantage of the line by picking Minnesota and winning, as Minnesota went on to win by 21 points. When a line does not fully take into account injuries, missing players, and hot and cold teams—and moves by only one to 3 points—but these factors often lead to 10 to 20 point differences, you have a betting opportunity.

In summary, the lines are set up in the sports gambling world in the hope that the bookmakers will be able to receive an equal amount of bets on each side of a given wager. The lines are not always a true value of the quality of the teams at the time of the wager. Public perception is a strong factor in making the lines. This factor then creates spreads, which are not always accurate. Use your sports knowledge and common sense to clearly see when some spreads are off, and then take advantage if you like the wager.

6. ANALYZE WAGERS FROM BOTH SIDES OF THE COIN

When making a wager, you must look at it from both sides of the coin. When I first started betting, I would look at a wager I liked and factor in only the positive aspects of the bet. But what I learned through experience was to analyze the positive aspects versus the negative points. Are the negative aspects powerful, or do they have little substance?

There are four types of bets you can make.

   a. You analyze a game in depth, and find a lot of evidence to support your wager. Then you place your bet knowing that you have a solid bet. You win the bet. Your research came through and the bet went as expected.

   b. You analyze a game in depth and find a lot of evidence to support your wager. Then you place your bet knowing that you have a solid wager. Unfortunately, the game or bet did not go as planned and you ended up losing the bet.

Here is an example that illustrates "b." I once bet on wide receiver Rod Smith, one of the best in the league, to make more catches than a pitcher's strikeouts that day. It was a fantasy prop bet. I researched the bet thoroughly and found that the receiver averaged five catches a game while the pitcher only averaged four strikeouts a game. The receiver was +2 in the spread. The bet looked great because the pitcher had just returned from the DL and I knew that he would only get so many innings in his first start after coming back. The pitcher almost never got more than six strikeouts in a given game. Therefore, if the pitcher got about his average of four strikeouts, all I needed was Smith to make two catches to push my bet, and three catches to win it. The bet looked great on paper.

What happened? The pitcher had only four strikeouts, so all I needed was two catches to push. Smith made his first catch in the first quarter. But on that play, he got hit late and threw a punch at an opposing player. Accidentally, he brushed the referee and was ejected from the game. This was a perfect example of a good wager that went bad. It was a rare occurrence, for I knew that it was a great pick and that I would win or push eight times out of ten. I had to live with the loss, knowing that I could not control the events that occurred. It was a good wager went bad due to some negative circumstances. It happens!

   c. You do not research and carefully think through a bet. You make a bet based on only a little information, or you make a hunch bet or a bet to get back at previous losses. It's a force bet that, luckily, turns into a winner. You have to minimize these types of bets because in the long run, you will not profit with them.

   d. You do not research and think through a bet very well. You make a hunch bet, or a bet to get back at previous losses. It's a force bet that ends up losing. This is the worst bet you can make! You know that it was based on nothing but you bet it anyway, and you lost. You look back and say, "What was I thinking?" You must minimize these types of wagers.

Here's a good example of how "c" and "d" bets often come about. Suppose your buddy Bob calls you to go to the bar to watch Monday Night Football. Just for the sake of betting, you decide to place a significant wager on the game because you are going to the bar to watch it.

If you can make most of your bets high-percentage wagers, you can win the majority of them. Meanwhile, minimize the poor bets you make—in fact, you should eliminate them altogether. Remember that it is your self-control as a sports handicapper that wins out in the long run. You choose what you bet on, not the house. If you are patient, you will find a lot of good and great bets if you know your sport and do the proper research. The basic winning philosophy is simple, yet few people follow it. Why make a wager that could go either way when, instead, you can wait a few days or even a week, find a great bet, and just wager more on that bet?

Thinking back, have you ever felt stupid by putting $300 on a sure bet you loved and won, and then lost $300 the next day on a bet you did not like that much? Don't allow this cycle to happen.

7. MAINTAIN YOUR DISCIPLINE

As I briefly touched upon earlier, discipline is an important factor in determining your success as a sports gambler. Do not bet with emotion just because you had a bad day betting on the Sunday football games and your three picks lost. Don't try to make it all back by guessing the winner on Monday Night Football. Look back at the picks you made on Sunday, determine where you went wrong, and try to learn from your mistakes.

Maybe it was just bad luck. Take your loss and be patient; good picks will soon be coming to you. If a friend tells you he has a great wager, it's okay to listen to what he has to say and ask him why he likes the pick. However, always look into it yourself from both sides and decide whether there is enough substance to take that pick. If not, do not take it.

Have the discipline to go days without making any picks, maintaining your self-control. Always think long-term, remembering that at the end of the year, you want to show a profit.

8. LEARN FROM YOUR MISTAKES

Nobody is perfect. No matter what you do, you are going to make some mistakes. If you have lost a couple of big bets, look back at them and the reasons you liked them at the time. Maybe you overlooked some factor that came into play and haunted you. Or maybe you actually made a great pick, but by misfortune or misplay, you happened to have lost. I have made many mistakes as a sports handicapper, but I have tried to learn from them. As a result, I am a better sports handicapper today than ever before.

When you analyze a wager, remember some of the mistakes you have made in the past to see whether they could be present in your analysis of your current pick. For example, suppose you decide to take the Washington Redskins over on the year in regular season wins at 8 1/2 games. You believe the team is loaded with talent, so you might make your wager in July before the preseason. Then in preseason games, they go 0-4. They lose their starting quarterback for seven games with a knee injury, and finish the regular season 4-12. A losing wager, yes, but what have you learned from it? Maybe you learned not to judge a team on its big-name talent, and maybe you should wait till after the preseason to see how the team is clicking. And perhaps you should make sure the team is healthy before wagering on it for regular-season wins. Some mistakes can be as simple as underestimating a team's quarterback.

Or, maybe you got burned betting big money on an NBA second half under. You were looking very good until the final moments of the game, but nine free throws were made during the last minute, and you lost your bet.

Don't be afraid of making mistakes as a sports gambler. Risk is involved with every wager you make. The key always comes down to the risk-versus-reward ratio. If you are too afraid of making mistakes, you will not win any money. You must live and learn from your mistakes. Just try to avoid making the same mistakes you have made in the past to help save yourself money in the future.

9. TAKE PICKS FROM FRIENDS

Some people say that in sports gambling, you must live and die with your own selections. I find this advice to be far from true. Maybe a friend of yours has information about a certain game that you do not have. Maybe he knows that a player is injured or got suspended, or maybe your friend is an expert in over/unders in basketball. Perhaps he specializes in a sport you know little about. Or maybe you have been so busy that you did not have time to get the inside scoop on a certain game.

If a friend calls and tells you he has a great pick, first ask him who he likes. Then, more importantly, ask him *why* he likes his pick. If he gives you good reasons to believe that he has a good pick, research the game to see if *you* really like it. Is the information your friend giving you for real? Or is he just making this selection based on bias or personal hunch? Don't consider the good or bad picks your friend has given you in the past, although his credibility as a sports gambler is a significant factor. Just look at the game itself and the info and reasoning he is giving you. After looking at the information carefully, it is up to you to make the final decision. Don't be afraid to stand pat and not take the selection. The bottom line is that you have to figure out if this bet is worth making.

Even if the last two wagers he gave you were winners, analyze the new wager rather than basing it on whether your friend is hot or cold. You may decide to put a very small wager of $50 on the game while your friend bets $400. Don't worry afterwards whether the bet ended up a winner or loser; anyone can flip a coin and call heads twice in a row. Just think beforehand whether it is a good or great wager. If it is, bet on it; if isn't, don't bet it.

Win or lose, it is your final decision to bet or not bet on that particular game. Thank your friend if the pick wins, but do not blame your friend if the pick loses. You were the one who risked your valuable money on it; ultimately, it was your call.

To conclude this tip, information is the key to making all your selections. Whether TV, radio, or friends, take it all in and then analyze it before making your selections.

When I see experts on television or radio give their picks on game day, it only means something to me if they can back up their picks with solid information or reasoning. I know right away whether their opinion and information is good, or if it is meaningless. If Jimmy Johnson is on TV and states that he likes the Steelers today in a big playoff game, it means nothing to me. I want to hear *why* he likes the Steelers. Then I may take his reasoning factors into consideration to make my own decision.

When experts give you opinions on television, always listen more to the why than the what. Don't be afraid to bet against their pick: They often make picks based on hunches. You know better than to do that! It is your money on the line, and you should make your final decision based on your own analysis.

10. STICK TO YOUR STRENGTHS AND SUCCESSFUL STYLE

To be a successful sports bettor, you need to focus on your strengths and limit your weaknesses. If your strength is in betting on college basketball, then make most of your bets in that sport. If your strength is wagering on football and baseball, stick to those sports. If you are better when betting on the money line than the spread, stick to wagering on the money line. If you are not good at picking over/unders, do not wager on over/unders. You have to go with what you are successful at.

If you want to expand your knowledge of different sports, start watching them on television and following box scores and re-caps to increase that knowledge. Do not wager on a sport until you have enough knowledge about it, and you are comfortable with the reasons you are placing bets in that sport. These factors will help you to reach your goal, which is long-term profit in that sport.

Suppose a friend comes to you with a great pick in boxing, a sport that you are not very familiar with. Do not suddenly place a large wager on it simply because your friend says it's a great pick. You must take the time to research the boxers' records, analyze the current match and previous matches, and analyze other key information before you can place an honest wager. If you do not know boxing at all, you should skip the pick. Always take what friends say with a grain of salt. Look into the wager calmly from both sides, even though your friend may sound excited over the phone because he thinks he has a steal. Stay calm and listen to the advice. You have to be able to determine whether he has meaningful information or is passing on hearsay and nonsense.

You will develop your style as a sports gambler based on what sports you are good at. Look back at your past bets, note where you have had success, and stick to that style. A friend's style might be to pick five football games every week, and bet money on all of them. This method might work for him, but maybe you would be better off betting bigger money on the one or two football picks you really like. Don't be tempted by stories of your friends winning money with parlays, for example. Everybody talks about their winnings, but they don't talk about their losses. Do not start betting on hockey because the basketball season hasn't yet begun; bet on hockey because you have the knowledge and because it fits into your style of betting. Stick to your successful ways and you should continue to be successful.

11. KEEP A RECORD OF YOUR SPORTS GAMBLING HISTORY

A very important component of your sports gambling career is keeping an accurate record of your financial gambling history. There are two charts that I recommend keeping.

DEPOSITS/WITHDRAWALS CHART

The first chart is a must for all sports gamblers and one that is easy to do for keeping track of the deposits or withdrawals into or from your sports book. It is a simple yet effective way to keep track of your sports gambling finances. This type of chart is excellent because not only will it help you monitor how much you are up, it will help you keep a record of all your transactions. If you send money by credit card or by Western Union, you can match and track your transactions in your gambling chart to your credit card/bank statements. Here is an example of what this chart should look like.

Date	Money Type	Book	Deposit or With-drawal	Amount	Running Total
01/15/04	XYZ Visa	MVP Games	Deposit	$7,200.00	-$7,200.00
02/11/04	Check	Magic Sports	With-drawal	$9,500.00	+$2,300.00
03/05/04	Check	MVP Games	With-drawal	$2,000.00	+$4,300.00

This simple chart is all you need to keep track of your financial ups and downs. The basics are the date, the money type (credit card, check, money order), the sports book name, deposit or withdrawal, amount, and running total. If you want to add extra features to your chart, you can list service charges and other details. Once you make your chart, keep the file on your computer for easy reference. It will only take a few minutes a month to keep track. If it takes more time than that, you are depositing and withdrawing too often and may be paying too much money in service charges.

When depositing and cashing out of sports books, you want to minimize the amount of service charges you pay because they can eat up your profits! Most good sports books will pay the transaction fee for you if you send money, though they usually require it to be over a certain amount. Western Union is a good way to send money if the sports book is willing to cover your fee. If depositing money by credit card, try to make sure that your credit card company will not charge you a service fee for sending money to a sports book. Also, try to minimize any fees charged by your sports book for credit card transactions.

You also want to minimize the fees you pay when you cash out of sports books. Most sports books will pay you by check in your country's currency, or U.S. currency depending on the sports book. The other option is for them to Western Union you the money, but that usually costs a high fee. The four most common methods are:

Western Union	(same day or next day)
Express Mail	(two to five business days)
Online Refund	(Bank Wire, two to three business days)
Regular Mail	(one to six weeks)

Most sports books will charge you either nothing or a very small fee for receiving a check by regular mail. For express mail, some sports books charge nothing, while others charge up to $40. Some sports books offer you one free cash-out per month. My recommendation is that, if you have money in the bank and are not in dire need of funds, you are better off taking the money by regular mail and saving the usual $24 in service fees. Why should you pay money in service fees when you can be using that money for something else that is important? As long as you believe that your regular mail is reliable and you know that you will get your money, you are better off waiting.

Actually, it depends on the amount that you are cashing out as well. On average a good savings account will pay you $2 to $3 a month in interest for every $1,000 you have in the bank. So if you are cashing out only $2,000, you might as well take it by regular mail, because that amount over four weeks will only gain about $5 in interest in your savings account. Certainly it makes no sense to pay $20 to $40 to be able to make that $5. Don't look at it and think, "I'm cashing out $2,000, what's $30?" What if the $2,000 is only $700 in profit, and what if last month you lost $400? Now you would be paying $30 out of recent winnings of only $300, or 10 percent of your win. Why give money away? Make the best financial move for your purposes.

On the other hand, if you need money right away for other purposes, you may have no choice but to eat the service fees and get the money by express mail.

DEPOSIT BONUSES

Some sports books will give you a 10 percent bonus on deposits. Try to take advantage of bonuses when you can; however, never make a bet because it will entitle you to a bonus. Only make bets when you find sound wagers. Deposit bonuses can be good, but some are very restrictive. Some sports books want you to roll them over four times or so in order to earn that bonus. Don't make $2,000 in bets simply because you want to clear your $200 bonus. Only look to acquire bonuses when it fits into your wagering plans, but before doing so, make sure you clearly understand the bonus rules. Take advantage of as many bonuses as possible when they make sense.

RESULTS CHART

The other kind of chart I recommend making is one that records all your wagers before an event, and the results of your wagers when the event has ended. It will only take minutes a day. This type of charting is important so that you can look back at all your wagers and see where you have made your mistakes and where you have been successful. With this knowledge, you can make a large portion of your bets in that sport or with that kind of wager.

The main purpose of this chart is to give you the ability to reflect on your past wagers. At the end of each sports season, tally your monetary wins and losses in each specific type of bet and sport. Record that number so that you can see how you have done and what to change for next season.

Recording your results is a must! How can you know how you are doing financially if you do not keep track of your results? Unless you record your wagers and results, you may think that you are up money, but not realize that you are not doing as well as you thought, or vice versa.

Recording all your bets is an excellent way to learn about yourself. Many sports gamblers don't realize what they are good at betting; they just make bets that they think are good without knowing their past records for these kinds of wagers. For example, you may be good at picking NBA home teams on the money line, while a friend may be good at finding good under bets in the NBA. Someone else may specialize in props, while others may concentrate on betting on tennis or NFL over/unders. Recording your wagers will help you maximize your strengths and learn from your mistakes by reviewing your results. A simple chart can look something like this.

Date	Sports Book	Amount	Sport	Type of Bet	Actual Wager	Result $Win/ Loss
12/15/04	MVP Wagers	$200	NBA	Proposition	Shaq O'Neal over 21.5 points	Win
12/27/04	Bookies R Us	$700	NFL	Over/Under	KC/Seattle over 45.5 points	Win

By learning your strengths and weaknesses, you may stay away from bets that lose you money and emphasize ones that are successful for you. For example, suppose you bet big money in the NFL on a team to win over 7 1/2 games. Shockingly, their star quarterback gets injured in the preseason and misses twelve games. They finish the season at 5-11. When next year comes around and you find a great bet you like in the NFL, you may still bet on it, but you might do so after the preseason. After seeing what happened in the past, you may realize that not only do injuries in the NFL happen frequently, but you also underestimated the strength of your team's schedule.

In addition to doing what you should do to become successful at sports handicapping, it is important to avoid doing things that will hinder your progress. In the next section, we'll take a look at nine things that profit-making sports bettors don't do.

CHAPTER 6

9 DON'TS FOR SUCCESSFUL SPORTS HANDICAPPERS

1. DON'T BET JUST BECAUSE THE GAME IS ON TV

As a sports gambler, always remember that you are wagering on sports for the main purpose of making money. Any secondary enjoyment you may get out of wagering must stay secondary, and not get in the way of your main goal, which is showing a long-term net profit.

The betting public likes to wager on primetime games. They enjoy getting in on the action and will make a wager on a game if it is televised, even if they do not strongly like one pick over another. For example, Monday Night Football is one of the most highly wagered sporting events in the world, with millions if not billions of dollars changing hands between bookmakers and gamblers during these games. But the question I ask is, "What makes this game more favorable to wager on than the 4:00 p.m. Sunday game between the Detroit Lions and Indianapolis Colts?" The answer, of course, is that it is not necessarily more favorable. It's just that a Monday night game is the only football game being played that day. And also, people often chase their Sunday losses on Monday night.

Don't think like the betting public thinks. Bet on a game only if you like the wager. Whether the game is being nationally televised should have no bearing on whether you bet it. You have no control over the outcome of the game once it commences, so whether you are watching it or not should not be a factor. I take a look at the football games each week, and if the Monday Night Football game does not do anything for me, I will not take it. I won't bet it even if I have lost money the day before. Bookmakers get rich by the public wagering on primetime games. At the end of the game, the bookmaker will collect the juice and be ahead of you if you think like the regular public.

My main point is to never bet just for the sake of betting. Bet only when you believe that you have a distinct advantage or value over the spread.

2. NEVER FALL IN LOVE WITH A TEAM

You cannot become emotionally attached to one team and believe that they will always win money for you. Wager with your head, not your heart. It is okay to ride a team's hot streak or to bet against a team's cold streak. If you find a trend on a certain team it is good to take advantage of that, just like I did with the Miami Heat's cold streak in 2007-2008.

However, don't bet on the San Francisco 49ers because you recall that they have always made money for you in the past and you think they will do it again. The thing to remember is that the players that have made money for you in the past may or may not still be on that team. Every game is a new game, teams change every year, player rosters change constantly. An 11-5 team one year can be a 5-11 team the next year. Never fall in love with one team; analyze each game within itself.

3. DON'T BET FOOLISHLY ON YOUR FAVORITES

Do not mix your head with your heart. Your heart may love your favorite teams, and your heart may try to convince your head that betting on them is a good wager, when it may not be. You must realize that you will be biased positively toward your teams and may end up wagering on them even though they are not as good as you think. I have a favorite team in all four of the major sports. After seeing my teams win some big games and blow a lot of games over the years, I actually am extra careful when betting on them.

My advice is to be careful: You may love and trust your teams so much that you become overconfident and bet on them expecting them to win every time. The key is to use all the extra information you know about your teams to your advantage when placing wagers, whether for or against. A lot of sports fans know their teams so well that they know whether or not the absence of a key player will affect the team. Don't be afraid to bet against your favorite team if you think they are overmatched. It won't hurt you if your team loses a regular season game, especially when you collect money!

Do not allow your emotions to take control of your brain. If you find that you are too biased when it comes to your teams, stay away from wagering on their games. You might not realize that with all the local coverage of your home team, you can be almost brainwashed into believing that your team is better than it is.

If you find that you are consistently biased in favor of your favorite teams, but are not making money by wagering on them, stay away from them and look elsewhere.

4. NEVER ASSUME ANYTHING

Assumptions without proper research can lead to disastrous bets. I have learned the hard way early in my career to never assume anything without really digging into the facts. Just because this and that have happened in the past doesn't mean that they will happen again. For example, don't assume that just because a team is playing at home, they will beat their opponent. Or, in a playoff series, don't assume that if a team has lost game one at home, they will bounce back and win game two. Yes, teams that are up against the wall often play better, but that doesn't mean they will.

Often the people who like to regularly wager on the favorites are in shock when a big favorite with the spread loses the game outright. Big upsets occur when one of two things happens, and sometimes both. It is actually quite simple.

Big upsets happen when poor, average or just good athletes and/or teams step up and play to their full potential on that day, while the great players and/or teams play below their potential and/or struggle miserably on that day. Any given day this can happen.

Big upsets happen when Vegas puts out a spread that is off on a given sporting event, and people with good knowledge take advantage of it and their pick ends up winning.

An example of a wrong assumption happened when the Denver Broncos beat the Green Bay Packers in the 1998 Super Bowl. Fans assumed that Green Bay was going to win the game. In reality, Denver was equally as talented. In my opinion, that win was not a shocker. It was a shocker in Vegas, but not to people who really knew the NFL.

Another good example of a wrong assumption in a series occurred during the 2003 Baseball World Series between the Florida Marlins and New York Yankees. A lot of the general public assumed that after New York beat Boston in a tough seven-game series, they were going to beat Florida. New York was a moderate money-line favorite in Vegas to win that series, and I know that millions of dollars were lost when Florida upset New York in six games. Especially in baseball, you cannot assume anything, because baseball is not a sport where a dominating team necessarily wins. Any team or player can step up in baseball and create an upset.

The bottom line is to never assume that certain things *will* happen. Always do your work and make good bets.

5. DON'T GET UPSET OVER UPSETS

In one game, anything can happen. If you look back through the history of sports and review all the great playoff upsets, you will find that the greatest ones occurred in single elimination games. In a best-of-seven-series in basketball or hockey, however, the better team will usually come out on top.

In the NCAA basketball tournament, there are many upsets every year because games are played on a neutral court and it comes down to which team played their A-game for 40 minutes on that day. Look to take advantage of high spreads in the NCAA tournament and bet on underdogs because, when there is no home court advantage, a lesser team can often keep a game close. The key with betting underdogs is to find a lower-ranked team that is just as talented as the higher-ranked team. Find a 12-seed that is just as talented as the 5-seed and bet on that team. Maybe the 10-seed is just as talented as the 2-seed, but you get +8 points to work with. You'll find many good opportunities in the NCAA tourney.

One of the biggest upsets of all time happened in 1980, the "Miracle on Ice," when the U.S.A. beat Russia in a semi-final Olympic hockey game to advance to the finals where they defeated Finland for the gold medal. Most hockey fans would agree that if they had faced the Russians in a seven-game series, the U.S.A. team would have had no chance of defeating them. Remember North Carolina State over the Houston Cougars with Clyde Drexler and Akeem Olajuwon? Or how about Villanova defeating Georgetown for the NCAA basketball title?

Other examples of upsets include the Super Bowl when Joe Namath predicted victory over the Baltimore Colts (and won), and when the New England Patriots defeated the St. Louis Rams. St. Louis was a 14-point favorite in that game, but lost by three. St. Louis was a great team that year with a good combination of defense and offense, but New England pulled off the upset with some timely special teams' play and defense.

In all these examples, I believe that the underdog was not good enough to win four times. That is why, in looking back at the NBA Playoffs for the past 20 years, there have been few upsets. And with the change of the first-round format from a best-of-five to a best-of-seven series, there will be even fewer in the future. Back in 2001, the Los Angeles Lakers faced Philadelphia in the NBA Finals in a best-of-seven series. If the series had ended after one game, Philly would have won the championship since they upset Los Angeles in game one of that series! Was anyone on the Lakers team worried? Not really, because they knew they had the better team. And they went on to win the next four games, three in Philadelphia.

My main point is that in one game, the better team will not always win. You have to recognize chance as a factor and consider the probabilities in your wager. This is why you never should bet too much on one contest.

6. DON'T FORCE BETS TO RECOUP LOSSES

Forcing bets to make up for lost wagers is one of the worst things you can do. For example, suppose you had a bad week and lost $2,500. The next week, you find a wager that you like a little bit and make a big bet to try to win back the $2,500. Moves like that can lead to a disastrous chain of events, which turns you into an emotional gambler who is out of control. Losing can be very emotional, more emotional than winning.

To be successful at sports betting, you must look at each wager as a brand new pick, without being influenced about past losses. If you are patient, and make good bets, you can recoup your losses. Don't look to find a quick fix. Just relax and live to fight another day.

At some point, everyone has chased losses and made bets they should not have made. Many years ago, this happened to me. Some of my forced bets turned out okay, but some lost. I recall thinking how lucky I was not to have been hurt badly in that stretch. Now I am in control of my wagering. If I take a hit, I look patiently to find some good or great wagers to get back on track.

An amateur gambler will get rattled, whereas a professional will keep his/her composure and find a way to win in the long run. Always think like the professional gambler.

7. BET THE GAME, NOT THE SPREAD

You will be looking at many different available wagering lines. You may see a spread that you feel is off. For a hypothetical example, suppose the Charlotte Bobcats at home against the Memphis Grizzlies are 5 1/2 point favorites. As an NBA follower, you think the spread should be Charlotte at -1 or -2 only. If they played 100 times, you think that Memphis would cover that spread about 60 of the 100 times. But the question you have to answer is whether you think they will cover *today*. If so, why? Or if you see an over/under line in the NFL that is at 42 1/2 and you think it should be 45 or 46, does that mean you have ample reason to bet the over?

Even though you think a spread is wrong, you shouldn't necessarily wager on it. You can't just bet the line, you have to bet first on how you think the game will go. For example, if you think a line is off by 2 or 3 points, you don't necessarily have a strong wager. If the line suits your way of thinking, then you bet on it. Besides the spread, you still must like the bet, and therefore, take advantage of the line that goes with it! Just because I think a spread is off does not mean that I am going to place a bet and feel confident that my side will win.

I look for individual wagers in which I feel I have an advantage, and the line offered correlates with my game on that day. So, if the spread is off, it does not mean that Charlotte cannot easily win the game by 6 points or more; and it doesn't mean that you should be confident in betting on Memphis or the NFL game to go over. If you see a spread that you think is off, look for reasons why you think that betting against that spread is a good move. If you have ample reason, then you should bet; if not, you should pass.

I would much rather bet a -250 that I feel strongly about than a +115 that I'm less confident with. Smart wagering is all about putting your money in advantageous wagers, not putting your money in when you find a bad spread. Now, don't get me wrong. You make money as a sports gambler by beating the spread, but you are looking for spreads you can take advantage of. Of course, you have to like the spread, but more importantly, you have to like the game or team or player.

8. DON'T FOCUS ON PAST STATISTICS

An important factor in sports wagering is to use information and statistics that are current and relevant. Statistics such as, "The Seattle Supersonics have won 68 percent of their home games over the last seven years against Eastern conference opponents" mean almost nothing. Those stats were based on different teams, different years, and different players. If Seattle is 8-2 at home this season, that statistic means something because it demonstrates that they have been a good home team so far *this* season.

Another example of a useless piece of information would be when the preview of a football game between the Green Bay Packers and the New York Jets states that Green Bay is 9-2 lifetime against New York. Do not be fooled by this statistic as it came from past teams and past players. The point spread for the game will be based on entirely different factors. Other meaningless stats are, for example, "The team that wins game five in a series wins the series 85 percent of the time." If the series is at 3-2, all it means is that one team has to win one game, while the other team has to win two games to win the series. Don't forget that a lot of series end in five games, so that is part of the 85 percent equation. If a team is down 3 to 2, or is up 3 to 2, that is all it means.

Other meaningless info that might be, "Bill Parcells is 14-5 lifetime coaching against his old teams," or maybe, "The San Francisco 49ers have the best winning percentage of all time on Monday Night Football." It is useless because this game involves different players on a new Bill Parcells team. And the reason the 49ers may have the best percentage is because they were a dynasty team during the 80s and 90s. If they are not a good team presently, they may be a legitimate dog in the game.

9. BEWARE OF BETS WHERE ONE PLAY CAN BEAT YOU

There are many bets that you can make in which one play can cause your wager to be a loser. Almost all these bets are some kind of proposition bet. The most basic example is betting on the coin toss in the Super Bowl. One simple toss will make you a winner or loser after one play. This is not a wager you want to make. Another example is taking a running back under 65 1/2 yards. In his first five carries, he might gain only seven yards, but then he could have one big run of 60 yards and that's it— your bet is ruined because of one play. The same goes for wide receivers.

Yet another example is betting that the longest field goal will be, let's say, under 43 1/2 yards. Or wagering on how many 3-pointers Tony Parker will make when the line is .5. You may like the under or the over, but he may take only one or two 3-point attempts per game, and your bet will depend on the outcome of those one or two shots. Another prop bet is how many blocks Shaq will have when the line is at two. You might look at the stats and notice that in the last five games, he has had at least two blocks. But would it shock you if, in this game, he finishes with only one or even zero blocks?

These are just a few of the many prop bets I could list that are subject to the one-play danger.

If you make wagers that are largely determined by one play, chances are that the outcomes of your bets will be very unpredictable. At times, these one-play bets can be good if you find the right proposition with them—but you have to be careful. You can't put big money on bets that come down to one play and feel very confident in your bet, regardless of what the stats say. You are safer betting on a full game, where a series of plays will make you right or wrong after the game.

On the other hand, if you can take a running back over by 65 1/2 yards and you know he will get at least 14 carries, if not 15 or even 20, then you may have a good bet. Why? Because even if he is struggling, your bet is always one play away from winning! These are bets where a series of plays can make you a winner, or one play can make you a winner. With these bets, you are putting yourself in a good position to win your wager.

Again, bet with extreme caution with the types of wagers that can make or break your bet in one play. Look at the statistics, but do not overanalyze them. More importantly, use your common sense and bet the proper unit amount. In sports gambling, whenever you are making a bet based solely on stats and percentages, you want those stats to clearly give you a huge percentage edge—or there is no point making that wager. For example, suppose you are thinking of taking Kyle Korver at over 1 1/2 three-pointers made for a game. You see that he has hit at least two 3-pointers in 55 percent of the games he has played so far this season. That is not enough. If you see that he has hit at least two 3-pointers in 65 to 75 percent or more of the games he has played on the season, *that* means something.

Now let's move on to a proactive approach to making your wagers. Next up is an important section that lists seven essential things to look for when analyzing the spread.

CHAPTER
7

7 THINGS TO LOOK FOR IN THE SPREAD

The following seven factors are the most important ones you should look for when checking spreads. They can help you break down a potentially good wager. As always, you're looking for bets that stand out. If nothing stands out, take the day off. When looking at statistics, you must always determine whether the information is current or is from the past. Current information you use, past information you don't. Here is a list of the key *present* information you are looking for.

1. WHO IS INJURED?

2. WHO IS HOT? WHO IS COLD?

Hot and cold is a meaningful concept. When one team is clicking and playing well, they are hot. When they are not clicking and not playing well, they are cold. The hot team has confidence, teamwork, and talent. The players know what each person's role on the team is, and they are doing what the coaches ask of them. The hot team is playing at its full potential.

The cold team is just not clicking and players are not playing to their potential. There are so many factors that are making the one team hot, while the same factors, albeit negative, are making the cold team cold. Hot and cold has true meaning in every sport. Hot/cold simply refers to whether a team is playing to its potential or not at a given time.

For example, suppose you are betting on a college basketball home team that has won 12 games in a row at home versus an opponent of equal talent. However, the opponent has lost two of its past four road games and you can get a money line of −145. It is probably a good bet, because in order for you to lose, the hot team will have to be defeated. For the most part, I will bet on hot teams and bet against cold teams. I rarely do the opposite unless I get a great point spread.

Never believe in the idea that one team is due for a win. There is no such thing. If a team is playing well, they have a better chance of winning their next game. If they are not clicking and are not playing well, they have a better chance of losing their next game.

3. WHAT ARE THE MATCHUPS LIKE?
Look for good overs or unders.

4. HAVE THE TEAMS PLAYED AGAINST EACH OTHER THIS SEASON? WHAT WERE THE RESULTS?

Don't use this as a primary guide to your bet, but it is a key factor to consider. Remember that the prior game could, just by coincidence, have been a low-scoring game because both teams combined to shoot 3 for 22 from the 3-point line. Analyze not only the box score, also read the recap to get a feel for what happened in the prior matchup.

5. ARE THEY A GOOD HOME TEAM? ARE THEY A GOOD ROAD TEAM?

In January 2004, the Dallas Mavericks were playing in Utah against the Jazz. The Mavericks were 3 1/2 point favorites because of their big-name talent, including Steve Nash, Dirk Nowitzki and Antawn Jamison. Dallas also had a recent history of success as a team. However, they were 4-11 on the road coming in, and Utah was 13-3 at home. With that information, there was no way that a sensible bettor could wager on Dallas. You either had to wager on Utah with their good home court play, or you didn't wager at all!

Utah won by 12, easily covering the spread as 3 1/2 point underdogs. Just by looking at the standings, I knew that I wasn't going to bet on Dallas. Simple information can go a long way.

6. WHAT KIND OF STYLE AND TEMPO WILL THE GAME HAVE?

This type of information can be found by watching the teams play and by looking at a team's recent box scores and recaps.

When a team makes a trade, they may suddenly go from a low-scoring team to a high-scoring team. When this happens, the team's statistics before the trade become useless because a new set of players is coming in. Here is a perfect example.

At the start of the 2003-2004 NBA season, the Chicago Bulls were the worst defensive team in the league, while the Toronto Raptors were one of the best. A trade took place in which the Raptors got three good offensive players in Jalen Rose, Donyell Marshall and Lonny Baxter, while Chicago got two defensive players in Jerome Williams and Antonio Davis. Chicago also hired a new, defensive-minded coach, Scott Skiles. Las Vegas, however, continued to make the over/under lines of their games fairly high, just as they were before the trade. I capitalized by wagering on Bulls' games under for the next couple of weeks as six of their next seven games went under. (The Toronto Raptors games became higher scoring affairs after the trade.) Eventually, Vegas adjusted the line to reflect the Bulls' new lineup. Once Vegas made the adjustment, I saw no edge, so I stopped betting the under in their games.

7. WHICH TEAM IS RESTED? WHICH IS NOT? WHO PLAYED LAST NIGHT?

A team that just took a long road trip or is coming off a grueling, exhausting game, can really suffer a drop off in performance. Always keep your eyes out for these opportunities.

Now that we've discussed the important factors to look for in the spread, let's take a look at seven strategies you can use to chalk up a profit at the end of every year. These winning strategies are key to your enjoyment and success at sports handicapping.

CHAPTER 8

7 STRATEGIES FOR WINNING

1. WHEN YOU FIND A GOOD SPREAD, TAKE IT

My first tip concerns the timing of your wagers. If you find a good spread, take it. If it is a good pick, the chances are good that the line will move against you as other sports handicappers also get in on the wager.

For example, if the night before a basketball game you see a spread come out on an over/under and you really like it, make the wager. Don't sleep on it because by the next day, the spread may move a point or so against you and you will have lost part of your wagering advantage.

Now, let's say that you find odds for the Kansas Jayhawks to win the national championship at 20 to 1. The team starts off the season 8- 0, and has beaten five ranked teams. If you like the pick, take it because the spread may move down to 7 or 6 to 1 within a few days.

Or you might look at the Jayhawks bet and say, "I want to see how they play in their next two road games against top-25 teams." That is a good way of thinking, because you are waiting for a reason to get a better feel of how good they really are. Only put off deciding on future spreads if you feel you need more information. Suppose you wager on an individual NFL game after you have done your research and analysis, and three days later, due to new information, you do not like the bet anymore. You always have the option to cancel out your bet (minus some juice) by wagering on the other side.

You always know when the lines will come out. The NFL games come out the Monday before the Sunday of the games. In the NBA and NHL, the lines come out the night before the games. In MLB the line also comes out either the night before the game or the day before it. When those lines come out, take a line if you really like it.

I am not stating that you should rush a bet; all your wagers have to be well researched and thought out. But if you have all your information at hand and like a bet, then make it and place that bet. I have found that the line usually stays or moves in a less favorable direction for me before game time. That's a sign of a good wager for I have received a spread at its peak.

Even if the line were to move against me, it doesn't shake my confidence. I don't believe in the theory that if the whole public is leaning one way, then it will probably be a losing bet or vice versa. I simply make my wagers as soon as I have gathered all the information and analysis that I need to make an intelligent decision.

2. BACK UP YOUR SPORTS KNOWLEDGE WITH STATS

Do not go to a sports website and try to find the lowest scoring team over the last five games and bet their next two games under. Why? Because you are looking at stats primarily to pick games for you. Stats are there to back you up, not choose for you. Your sports knowledge and logical reasoning is what will find games; the stats should only support your thoughts.

Often, you can take advantage by finding a spread that is based on past statistics, but you know that the spread is off. I once wagered over on an NCAA basketball game in the first half in a game between two solid scoring teams. The spread was very low because the first game they played against each other earlier in the season was very low scoring. However, that game was an aberration, not at all indicative of the high scoring games they almost always played. I easily won that bet, as the teams played with their routine good pace and play.

3. ACCURATELY INTERPRET LINE MOVEMENT

Line movement is a big part of the business of sports gambling. Figuring out how that should affect the wagers you make will help you maximize your profit as a sports gambler. First, I will discuss how the sports gambling market generally works with line movement, and then I will go over my recommendations on how to interpret line movements for your wagers.

Let me remind you that the line set up by Vegas and the sports books is designed to balance the amount wagered on each side of a given wager. The sports books would like to have, for example, $110,000 wagered on each side of a given game so that, either way, they will profit $10,000 in vigorish.

When the line comes out on a given sporting event, it is called the *opening line*. The *closing line* is the final line with a given sports book right before the game commences. The line in a sporting event is generally moved for two reasons:

It is reported or confirmed that a key player will not be playing in a given match due to injury or suspension; and

Significant money is being placed on one side of the wager.

During a sports season, players often miss significant time due to injury. The line set by Vegas and the sports books already incorporates the fact that a key player is not playing in a given game. However, during a season a player might be listed as questionable heading into a given match. In this situation, an opening line may come out late on a particular match, but as soon as it is reported and confirmed that a key player will not be playing, a basketball line, for example, can move anywhere from 1 to 5 points. The better the player, the more the points.

In one example of an NBA wager that I made, Steve Nash was questionable heading into a home game in Phoenix against the Spurs. Originally, the Suns were 1-point underdogs to win the game, but as soon as it was confirmed that Nash was not playing, the line moved 4 points to the Spurs minus-5. The sports books had to move the line to try to put a spread with a real value in the game and to ensure they didn't get killed as people started wagering against the injured team. Even though the line moved, I still bet big on the Spurs because I knew that Nash was the quarterback of the Suns and they would be in bad shape without him. Nash actually won the MVP that season, and the Spurs ended up winning the game in a blowout.

The website Covers.com has detailed injury reports. I suggest using them as a reference guide when making all of your wagers.

Here's another good tip for finding out one to two hours before a match whether a questionable player is playing. Suppose Lebron James is questionable for Cleveland and they are at home -2 points against the Portland Trail Blazers. If you suddenly see that the Cavaliers have become 2 1/2 point underdogs, you know that Lebron James will not be playing in the given match because the line has moved 4 1/2 points. Secondly, the line moves when there is significant money placed on one side of a given wager. This is referred to as a *steam move*. There are two sets of gamblers in the sports gambling world. The first set is the general public and the second one is the pros or the *wise guys*, as they are often called. A sports book will move a line if too much money is being placed on one side to try to make the other side look favorable for a wager. They then hope to balance their books. They are especially aware of where the pros are putting the money. If some pros are putting down significant money on a given side of a game, often a lot of the future action on a given wager is made on the same side.

When the line moves because of money being placed on a side, it is really only a small move. Half a point to 1 point movements are the norm, though sometimes you will see lines move by 2 to 3 points. The sports books generally do not move the lines more than a few points because it does not make much business sense for them.

The money line also moves, just as the point spread line moves, so be aware of that. Also, understand that since prop bets get less action than regular games, one significant wager can move the line significantly. A player whose points were listed at 19.5

points and over at -115 can move to 20 and over at -160 very quickly. Prop wagers always have more dramatic line changes because they are wagered less and thus are more vulnerable to movement.

The public often likes to wager on overs and favorites, and they generally make their wagers the same day of the game. Pro bettors, on the other hand, look to make a wager as soon as they see a favorable line, maybe five days before an NFL game is played.

Given all this information on line movement, how do you incorporate all this into your sports betting strategy? First, it is very important to have multiple sports book accounts open to ensure that you get the best line possible when you wager. You want to shop around for the best line. Half a point or 1 point can make the difference in a close wager, and a money line of -180 in one account and a line of -190 in another is significant and automatically benefits you.

Line movements due to injury are of major importance. Always look to potentially bet against teams that are shorthanded, even if the line has already moved to reflect the injured player. If Lebron James is not playing, you should not care whether you get +2, -1 1/2, or even -3. Depending on the quality of his team at the time, you should consider betting against his team almost every time when he is out. If the point spread has moved too much, look to bet against his team on the money line at -150, -200, or even -300. A win is a win, money in your pocket. Keep up with the injury status of certain players in order to jump on the lines before they move, or just as they are moving, to get the best line possible.

Steam moves or line moves due to heavy wagering on one side of a bet only have meaning because you are always trying to find the best line possible in the games you like. Never make a bet one way or another based on whether the public or the pros are putting big money on one side. You should not significantly care what other people are betting, care only on what you are betting.

Further, you should almost never back away from a wager if it has moved 1 point against you. You should care about the 1 point that you lost, but not enough to shy away from your bet. You should be looking to kill the line and win your bets by decisive margins. Just because a line has moved a point or two does not mean, for example, that Kobe Bryant is going to have a better game or that the Lakers have a better chance to win. All it means is that people are putting money on the Lakers. Don't be afraid to bet against where the line is going, and don't be overconfident or afraid of wagering on where all the money in a game is going. Always look at the real sports information as the reasoning behind your wagers, never what the market dictates.

Another key point is that, if you like a team in the NBA at -5 points and the line moves to -7 points, never look to change your mind and bet on the other team at +7 points. 2 points should never make you take the other side, although it can change your mind into not making the original wager because you don't like the new line. Making this type of move would mean that you didn't have any significant value or reasoning to begin with. Take the original wager or stand pat.

I don't recommend placing too much significance on the line movement. It should not be a direct reason you are wagering on one team over another. Your main way in making money as a sports handicapper is by betting on strength or against weakness in the appropriate sports match.

Let's look at an example of a wager involving line movement. On December 3rd, 2007, the Baltimore Ravens hosted the New England Patriots on Monday Night Football. The spread came out seven days before the game at New England -21 points. I loved Baltimore at +21 and made my bet as soon as I could at that number (which was three touchdowns). I doubted the line would move to New England -22 or 23, and I also believed that the line could most definitely move down to +18, 19, or 20. Before game time, the spread closed all the way down to New England -18. Baltimore ended up covering the spread easily anyway, losing 27-24. I knew that the spread was overinflated, and that most of the money would be bet on Baltimore. So, I got the spread I wanted at its peak.

As you gain experience as a sports handicapper, you'll learn to estimate in which direction the lines will move.

To recap this section on line movement, don't get too intrigued by the lines moving. Get the best spread you can on any given wager as soon as you have finished all your research on a given game, utilizing all sports books for the best deal. When a line is moving, try to figure out why. If it's because of the money wagered on one side, don't get excited by it. If it's because of a key player not playing, look to possibly take advantage and make a good wager in that situation. Your analysis on how a given sporting event will go means a lot more than the market and a small line movement.

4. MAKE QUALITY BETS, NOT A QUANTITY OF BETS

If you want to be a winner as a sports gambler, you must be selective in the games you choose, and have concrete reasons for making each wager. If you feel that you have a 50 percent chance of winning based on the point spread, remember you are risking -110. This is not good enough. Every time I place a bet on which I am laying at least -110, I like to think that I have at least a 60 percent chance of winning. If I thought my chances of winning were less than that, say 58 percent, I would not even bother making the wager. It is not enough of an edge to be profitable. Of course, these numbers are, subjective, but the point is you need a high level of confidence in your bets before you make them.

Most of the games out there I don't touch. Making three to four wagers every day is not a way to pull in a long-term profit. If you are making 15 to 20 wagers a week, even if you are pulling even on your picks and winning half of them, you will be losing so much money in juice you won't even realize where your money is going. For example, let's say you make 80 bets over a two-week period (which is way too many), win 41 of them and lose 39. You have won more bets than you have lost, but you would have lost money if you bet the same amount on each wager. If you wagered an average of $220 a game, you would take home $8,200 for the 41 games you won, but you would lose $8,580 on the 39 games you lost. Your net loss would be $380 during those two weeks.

The way to win money is to stick to the unit system of money management, remain patient, and be very selective in the games that you choose. Some weeks you might make only two wagers, other weeks maybe eight or nine. Never have a predetermined number of wagers—just make bets one at a time looking for edge and value. Discipline is your key to success. Don't get upset if you liked a game but decided not to pull the trigger on that wager and it won. This is a good sign indicating that you showed discipline by holding back on a game you semi-liked. As I keep stressing, being lukewarm on a game is a formula for losing. Further, it demonstrates that you had the ability to pick a winner, even though you did not bet on it.

Some new bettors think that great wagers do not show up that often, but that's not true. If you are patient you will see that great bets come up for as long as you keep up to date with your good sports knowledge. If you are making bets just for the sake of betting, you won't win in the long run. You have to be smarter than the average gambler, always remembering quality over quantity in making your wagers!

5. BET ON HOT TEAMS, BET AGAINST COLD TEAMS

"Winning cures everything" is a saying you often hear in professional or college sports. Well, winning may not cure everything, but it does cure a lot of things. When you are betting on an individual team, an important betting factor is how they have played in their last five or fewer games. When a team is winning and they are hot, everything seems to go right: Last-second bounces seem to go their way, they are healthy, playing as a unit, everyone is playing their role, and team chemistry is at a high. On the other hand, when a team is losing, last-second bounces do not go their way. Players have a lack of confidence and that affects results. For these reasons and others, you usually should bet on the hot teams and bet against cold teams, regardless of the spread. The bottom line is that hot teams are playing up to their potential, while cold teams are not.

The lines set up by sports books and Vegas do not fully take into account the hot streak of a team. For example, the Milwaukee Bucks were playing great basketball and had won nine home games in a row leading up to their home game versus New Jersey on January 15, 2004. The Nets were playing good basketball as well. But nine in a row at home is impressive, so the Bucks normally would be a pick with no spread. But because the Bucks were really hot at home, Vegas had the line established at the Bucks -2 1/2. As I stated earlier, 2 1/2 points in the length of a 48-minute basketball game is not a big deal, it is one 3-point shot. So, whether the Bucks are a pick or a 2 1/2 point favorite, they are a good pick for the night based on their recent success at home. Even if you had been unsure about the 2 1/2 points, you could have wagered on the money line to get a line of about -145.

The Bucks won the game and covered the spread, to make it ten home wins in a row. You could have said to yourself, "I will bet on Milwaukee. I'd like to make NJ try to beat them at home, a place where the Bucks have not lost in a while." If NJ had won, you would have had to give them credit, but they did not and the trend continued.

I call those kinds of bets, "Make them beat you" bets. Sometimes, if a team has won nine or ten games in a row, betting on them can be a good move as you are forcing another team to beat their streak.

The tennis great Rafael Nadal won 81 consecutive clay court matches in a row. Even though he was a big favorite in most of those matches, they were all winning wagers. By betting on Nadal, you were forcing a huge upset in order to lose your bet.

In another example, between 2003 and 2004 combined, the New England Patriots won 18 consecutive regular season games and 21 straight, including the playoffs. If you had bet the money line on them in every game, you would have won money!

It's a good formula: Bet on hot teams.

It works both ways: Be wary of betting on teams that have lost five or more games in a row. For example, in the 2007-2008 NBA season, the Miami Heat lost 21 of 22 games at one point during the season, yet there was still good value betting against them on the money line. In late January of 2008, I wagered on the Eastern Conference champion Cleveland Cavaliers at -165 on the money line in Miami (the actual spread was Cleveland at -3 1/2). Miami had lost 13 games in a row coming in, and Cleveland had started to play well. Cleveland had control of the game during the entire second half, cruising to victory, 97-90. This bet seemed too easy: I was betting against a terrible team. I really think the spread should have been at least 5 1/2 points with a money line of at least -240 on Cleveland. I successfully bet against Miami a few other times during their horrific 2007-2008 NBA season.

Do not get tempted by a generous spread. Teams that have lost five or more in a row are vulnerable to being blown out. Teams that are cold have injuries, bad chemistry, poor coach/player communication, low confidence and inferior talent. All these factors add up to a disgruntled, cold team. They are losing for a reason.

6. STANDING PAT IS OKAY

You should not bet on every game. If nothing catches your eye, pass. As a sports gambler, you must maintain the discipline to stand pat rather than betting on a match that you only like a little bit. Never feel that you have to place a wager on anything. Don't think that you missed an opportunity when a bet that you passed wins. If you really like a wager, take it; if you don't like it very much, don't take it.

Standing pat can be a great asset. If someone told you that you could make only 20 bets during the whole year, you would be selective and would win a lot more than normal. When you stand pat you are even; you don't win or lose money. Making a large quantity of bets just for the sake of being in the action gives the advantage to your bookmaker. Always look for quality over quantity. If you do, good wagers will come to you.

7. LEAVE ROOM FOR ERROR

In sports gambling, you want to win as high a percentage of your bets as possible so that you can show a consistent profit. Ideally, you would love to win most of your bets by 20 points in a cakewalk, and you might win a lot of your bets by big margins, but that is not what usually happens. Even when you find great bets, certain players or teams must play up to their expectations for you to win. To put yourself in a position to win as much as possible, you have to make bets that have room for error. Here is a hypothetical example.

Let's say that you have never watched an NCAA basketball tournament game in your entire life. A friend of yours wants to make a friendly wager with the loser buying the winner a beer. Wisconsin is playing Arizona on a neutral court in Georgia, and Arizona is favored by 9 1/2 points. Your friend tells you to pick whoever you want, either Wisconsin at +9 1/2 or Arizona at -9 1/2. If I were you, I would take Wisconsin at +9 1/2. Why? Because twelve college basketball players are playing against another twelve players on a neutral court. Take the 9 1/2 points and if your team plays well, you will always be in position to win. Even if they are down by 12 points with five minutes left, you are only 3 points away from winning your bet. On the other hand, if you take Arizona, they may not be in position to win even if they are down by one with seven minutes left.

I would almost never take any NFL game under less than 38 points because there is no room for error. The spread is just too low. Even if the teams both have great defenses and bad offenses, there can easily be interceptions returned for touchdowns; fumbles at the 10-yard line; or touchdowns by special teams. Two big plays and you're up against the wall! There is no room for error betting under 37 or less, no matter how bad the offenses are.

A perfect example of a spread that had no room for error was the 2004 Super Bowl between Carolina and New England. The total in the game was 38 points because both teams had great defenses. I thought the game would be low scoring, that a score of maybe 20-17 or 20-14 could be the final. Did I bet under? No. I didn't want to bet in a situation where my best-case scenario was winning by 4 points! With no room for error, I did not touch the over/under in the game.

During the first quarter, nobody could move the ball. It was scoreless, and the under was looking good for those bettors. However, after a couple of big plays, the game broke wide open. The final score went way over the spread, ending at 32-29 with New England on top. The teams scored a total of 61 points!

You should have the potential of winning your wagers by 20 points. If you bet under 38, you are hoping to win by a score of 20-14 or 17-10 or something like that, but you cannot predict when the big play will happen. On the other hand, if you bet any NFL game over 34 to 36, you should be in a position to win most of the time heading into the fourth quarter. The NFL is geared toward high-scoring games. All the new rules help teams' offenses, not their defenses, succeed. NFL defensive backs can barely touch a receiver downfield without being called for a penalty. Overall, you are never really safe with an NFL under bet until the game is over.

Another bet I almost never take is an NBA team to cover over 14 points, and rarely will I take any NBA team for a substantial bet at -11 or more. I may make an exception if there are substantial injuries in the game and I predict a blowout. With ten professional players, who is to say that the team that is +14 can't step up and keep the game close? Even if you take a team at +14 and they are down by 17 with five minutes left, the scrubs often will come into the game and your team can make a comeback during garbage time since no one is really playing with an eye on the scoreboard. In a perfect world, all of your bets would win easily, but we still have to put ourselves in position to win as often as possible.

On the other hand, I would make a bet at -600 on the money line, depending on what type of wager it is. If it's an award bet that I like, then why not? It would have to be a situation where a minor miracle would need to happen for me to lose. If I can take easy money at -600 and, barring a miracle, I strongly believe that I'll win, I'll take it. I would not take a team in one game at -600 very often, though I would take it in a series or in a special situation such as an Olympic event where one team is outclassed. I may also take it in a prop bet where I have a lot of room for error.

People look at NFL games every Sunday night and say, "Man, look at all of these upsets!" But were they really upsets? Football is a sport where a great player like Emmitt Smith can fumble a ball at the five-yard line, and the other team can recover it and run it back 95 yards for a touchdown, resulting in a 14-point swing. These types of things happen quite often, usually for 50 to 80 yard returns. Any player can fumble the ball and any great quarterback can throw an interception that gets returned for a touchdown.

There is so much parity in the NFL that, if you can take a decent home team at +5 1/2 points versus a non-dominant team, the bet might be profitable. Or, if you can take a road team at +10 points versus a non-dominant team, at least you have 10 points in your pocket to work with. If your team plays great, they may win the game. If they play well, they will cover the 10-point spread. If they play poorly, you may still win with a late TD, because even if they are down by 16 with two minutes left, your team can still drive downfield and cover the spread in garbage time.

Another good example of a bet that left room for error was in the 2005 Super Bowl between Philadelphia and New England. I bet money on Philly at +7 1/2 and -110. Two great teams were facing each other on a neutral field and I liked the wager a lot. At +7 1/2, I was forcing New England to have to win by two scores to make my wager a loser. I had room for error because Philly could win the game, they could lose a close one, or they could score late to get within a touchdown. The latter happened, as Philly scored a late touchdown and ended up losing by 3 points in a game that could have gone either way. Betting on New England at -7 would not have left room for error, I decided, because New England would have to win by two scores to win the wager. Most of the public took New England at -7 because they had blown out their previous two opponents in Pittsburgh and Indianapolis. The public did not realize how solid a team Philadelphia was. I knew that Philly was a great team, better than any team New England had played so far that season.

In another example, the New England Patriots were favored by 12 1/2 points on a neutral field against a great defensive team, the New York Giants, in the 2008 Super Bowl. I would never have taken the New England Patriots to cover. I can find great teams at home in the NFL regular season at -6 or -7 against terrible teams, so why would I take one great team to beat another great team at -12 1/2 points? Why would I take one conference champion to beat another conference champion at -12 1/2 points? The Giants were a solid wager to cover the spread and ended up winning the game outright 17-14.

The coach of the favored team does not care whether or not his team covers the points. His coaching and strategy is not designed to help you win your wager. It is designed to help him walk away with a victory, just like Belichick did against Philly in the 2005 Super Bowl.

Often you will find that an NFL team is not a dominant team, but it is favored by say, 8 points at home. They might be favored by 8 points because they are playing well so far with a record of 3-1. Any team can be 3-1 if they play decent football and get a little lucky or start out with a weak schedule. Suppose you come across an NBA doormat team that won only 28 games the previous year. The team has kept the same players as the year before, but they start out 3-1 in the current season. Would you bet on it at -9 points? Probably not. Four games are not enough of an indicator to determine how good a team is.

The betting public usually likes betting on favorites, but I prefer wagering on the better team (though the favorite usually is the better team). However, never underestimate the underdog. Try not to put yourself in a bet where you take a team at -9 points, and on the first series, the opponent's quarterback throws a 50-yard pass for a touchdown. Suddenly, you're down

16 points. If you're taking a team at -9 in the NFL, it is because you think your team will win by at least three touchdowns, not slide by with a 10-point victory. This is the way to think.

Give yourself a margin for error.

Does your bet allow for different ways for your team to cover the spread? Or are you in a position where almost everything must go the way you planned for you to win your bet? If it is the latter, think through your bet very carefully before making it.

In professional sports, there is a lot more parity than in college sports. The professional teams have the best players in the world, while, on given days, some college teams are playing against talent that is on another level entirely. Often, you will see a team in the NBA that is up by 15 points at the half go on to win the game by 9 points, for example. But a college basketball team that is up by 15 at the half might win the game by 28 points. Taking teams in the NFL at -18 points can be tough, or taking a team in the NBA at -14 points can be risky, because the football team could win the game 30-14, and the basketball team could be up by 18 late, yet end up winning the game by only 12 points due to garbage time.

Another example of not leaving room for error is betting an NBA game under 85 points for the first half. One hot quarter and you cannot catch up. A better wager would be taking the over on a game that has a favorable line. Sometimes, for example, you can find two efficient, offensive teams playing each other at a line of 180 for the game. With a line like that, you always have a chance when betting the over.

Put your bets in position to win; that is, don't force your teams to cover a spread that is too big, and don't bet the under on NFL games that have very low spreads. On the other hand, don't bet on a garbage team at +9 points in the NFL if they are totally outclassed. Use common sense to leave room for error in any sport or any league, thus giving your bets every chance to succeed. Good bets always leave room for error.

The next section explains seven types of bets that can bring you success as a sports gambler.

CHAPTER 9

7 WAYS TO WAGER

1. WAGER ON THE MONEY LINE

Betting on the money line can bring great opportunities, but it's *how* you bet the money line that determines your success. When you bet the money line, you eliminate the point-spread factor in a game. In other words, you pick a team to win the game outright without having to worry about a point spread. Suppose your team is a 6-point favorite and you are confident they will win, but you're not fully confident they will cover the spread. You can still win by betting the money line, as opposed to losing money betting the spread if your team wins by only 1 to 5 points. You can make money by betting on favorites with the money line at -200 or -300 or higher, and you can make money by betting the underdog on the money line at +200, 300, 400 or higher. The key with money-line bets is analyzing the line to get good value.

A good example of a money-line wager that I made occurred February 13, 2008, when the New Jersey Nets were at home against the Minnesota Timberwolves. The Nets were favored by 7 points and were -270 on the money line. Minnesota was 2-22 on the road, and Rashad McCants, their second-highest scorer, was injured and would not be playing. Minnesota had possibly the least talented team in the NBA that year, while New Jersey was underachieving, but was finally fully healthy and had won three games in a row at home coming into the contest. I loved New Jersey to win that game. I thought it was a very secure wager; however, I was unsure if they would cover the 7-point spread. I loved the money line bet, but did not touch the spread wager. Getting -270 on a decent team versus a team that wins only one out of every 11 road games they play was great. I also liked betting on Jason Kidd, Vince Carter and Richard Jefferson against a bunch of no-name players. All these factors gave me confidence.

So what happened? It was an ugly game! Minnesota's offense looked anemic and while New Jersey did not play their best game, they maintained a small lead most of the way and built a double-digit lead in the second half, hanging on to win by 4 points, 92-88. This is an excellent example of a wager that I would not have made with the spread, but loved with a money line of -270.

Remember that you want to make money over the long haul, so if you are betting on a -350 that you like a lot, you had better strongly believe that it's going to win because if your -350s start to lose, you are in big trouble!

I once bet on tennis player Marat Safin at -320. All Safin had to do was win the match. The other player was in over his head, and I gave him about a 1 percent chance of winning the match. Guillermo Coria, the player I bet against, had just come back from shoulder surgery and had played only one match in the last three months. In tennis, you need playing time to get back to 100 percent on your game so I didn't like his chances. Also, Coria was playing on a hardcourt, one of his worst surfaces, while Safin was on fire and was playing on his best surface. The only reason Coria was in this tournament was because he had racked up enough points on the year in clay tournaments to qualify for the Masters Cup. Coria got killed in straight sets 1-6, 4-6. It was easy money. -320 on a great bet is worth it compared to a -120 that may or may not win. Tennis can be a great sport to bet because it is straight player-versus-player with a money line. Your player doesn't have to cover any kind of spread; he just has to win the match.

Of course, in one game anything can happen. So, if you are betting on a -300 or -400, you have to really believe that only a shocking upset will make you lose. The only time I will bet on an NBA team at -400 or higher is when the other team is decimated by injuries or has a comparatively untalented team.

On the other hand, if two teams are playing each other in a best-of-seven series and I feel that one team is a huge favorite to beat the other at -300 or even -400, I will make that wager. Although I am risking a lot more to make a little, I have a lot more room for error, because the underdog team will have to beat me four games out of seven. Comparing individual games to a series of games, common sense dictates that it is much better to bet on something at -300 over a seven-game period because you have a lot of room for error. On the other side of the coin, it is much better to bet on a team at +300 in a one-game situation, because an upset is more likely to occur! I would rarely recommend taking a team at +250 to +350 to win a series. It doesn't make sense because you have to beat a better team four times to make money; you are better off taking your chances in one game.

Be very careful in betting big bucks on the money line in the NFL because the old axiom, "On any given Sunday," is so true! Football is a sport with a lot of variables. Tipped balls for interceptions, fumbles, injured quarterbacks, bad weather, bad calls, dropped balls—any and all of these single events can lead to major upsets! So, be very careful when betting on big favorites in the NFL at -300 or above, because many times the underdog will come through!

Week 7 of the 2004 NFL season is a perfect example of how underdogs are always dangerous. In this week, five 6-point underdogs or higher beat their opponents outright! The big favorites for the week went down like dominoes. Jacksonville, a 10-point underdog, won in Indy 27-24. Detroit, a 6 ½-point underdog, won against the Giants in New York, beating New York 28-13. St. Louis lost in Miami as a 6 ½-point favorite, 31-14. Seattle, a 7-point favorite, lost in Arizona 25-17. And on Monday night, Cincinnati, a 7-point underdog, won at home against Denver, 23 to 10. This all happened during one week! Parity is very real in the NFL, so be careful betting on big money-line favorites.

Whenever you give up more money to make less money, you should do so because you believe that you have a big advantage. If you like a bet at -300 but you don't *love* it, bet small. On the other hand, if you think that you have a great bet, push a larger bet out there. Always keep in mind that your advantage over the sports books is that you control how much and when you bet.

Betting underdogs can be a great way of making money on the money line, but it takes a lot of patience. Some of the best opportunities to bet on underdogs with the money line are the following:

- College basketball home teams
- NBA home teams
- NFL home teams
- Award bets or other props

In college basketball, home court advantage is probably more a factor than in any other North American sport for three main reasons:

1. College crowds are much louder than pro crowds. Students really bond with their teams and have enough energy to scream throughout the game. They make a big impact, giving the home team an advantage.

2. A college basketball team is made up of kids between 18 to 23 years old who often do not have the poise or maturity to keep their composure playing against a hostile crowd. As talented as a road team may be, it is sometimes difficult for them to overcome the home team's advantage.

3. Basketball is a game of runs. The home team has an advantage with a good crowd because it helps spur them on to make big runs during a game.

Obviously, a team needs some talent to win, so look for talented teams that are money-line underdogs at home, teams that may be underachievers. If you like the wager, take it. If you know college basketball, you definitely can make money wagering on it because so many games are played in one week, sometimes as many as 50 games in one night. However, you don't need knowledge of all the teams to be successful at betting it. Simply keep track of the top 25, and then expand your knowledge outside of this group. Most importantly, watch as many teams play as you can to get a feel for the strengths and weaknesses of different teams.

NBA home teams are always a decent bet in terms of money-line underdogs because almost any NBA team on any night can beat the road team if they just step up for the one game. It's simply a matter of finding the right game at the right time. During the NBA season, you often can find a team at home at +150 on the money line. Take a quick look at the standings and you might discover that this team is 20-12 at home on the season, while their opponent is 14-18 on the road. You often will see teams in the NBA as underdogs at home, even though they are much better at home than their opponents are on the road. Find the games you like and take advantage with a spread that might be off.

NFL games are excellent for betting money-line underdogs. The home-field advantage is huge. Sometimes, it also comes down to whether your team wins the turnover battle. If it does, your team will have a great advantage, and its odds of winning can make the money-line wager worthwhile. Look for under-achieving NFL teams that can steal a game, and you can win big at +300, +400, +500 or even higher! Baseball is also a good sport to bet on underdogs because there really are no upsets in baseball. Any team can beat any team on any night.

Here's another tip to use when you find a solid underdog pick. Let's say that you find an underdog college basketball team that is playing at home. You think they have been underachieving this season, and you see that they are 11.5-point underdogs at home. Looking at their opponent, you think that they have a decent chance of winning the game and should cover the spread easily. The money line in the game is +500. You bet $2,000 on the spread and make a smaller wager of around $300 on the money line. If your team plays the way you think they will and loses by between 1 and 11 points, you will win your spread bet. You will profit $1,818.18 ($2,000 divided by 1.10) minus the $300 you lost on the money line. You will profit $1,518.18 even if your team loses. If your team steps up and wins the game, you will win the $1,818.18 plus an additional $1,500 on the money line for a total profit of $3,318.18 after risking only $2,300.

In this situation, your spread bet protects your money-line wager. You are not afraid to risk $300 on the money line because you have a great belief that you will at least win your spread bet and be up in the game. You could also have bet $2,000 on the spread and $800 on the money line, or $1,000 on the money line, depending on how much you want to differentiate between the two bets. However, always bet more on the spread to ensure some profit.

You want to profit in every situation where you believe that you have an advantage so that you will enjoy long-term success. You would miss a good opportunity if you loved your team, but didn't touch the spread wager, and only bet $200 on the money line at +500. If the team lost by 1 to 11 points, you wouldn't have profited from a game that you loved. Bet bigger on the spread, and bet proportionately smaller on the money line. This way you can still show a profit when your team covers the spread but does not win outright.

When betting on money-line favorites and underdogs, bet proportionately. If you love a team at -300 in a big favorite to win, you may decide to bet $300 to win $100 because the other team has major injuries. On the other hand, don't bet $110 on an underdog at +140 that you think has a 40 percent chance of winning. In this scenario, if your big favorite wins but your underdog loses, you are still down $10 on the day. Even if your underdog wins and your favorite loses, you are still down $140 on the day, so you would have to win both bets in order to profit.

A better way to go about it is to wager $450 to win $150 on the favorite, and wager $40 at +140 on the underdog. If only your favorite wins, you are up $110, but if both come through, you are up $206. Always look to put most of your money on the wagers that you think are more secure to win regardless of betting on favorites and underdogs. Remember that with every secure bet you win, you are not only making money, you are protecting your capital. Winning money consistently on a daily basis will ensure long-term profit.

Below is a money line chart for beating the breakeven point in money line wagers.

MONEY LINE WAGERS	
-110 52%	+110 48%
-150 60%	+150 40%
-200 66%	+200 33%
-300 75%	+300 25%
-400 80%	+400 20%
-500 83%	+500 17%
-600 86%	+600 14%

If you take a bet at -300 or even at +400, the chart will help you understand whether or not the bet is worth making. If you are making a bet at -200, you have to believe that it has a more than a 2 out of 3, or 66 percent chance to win. Always aspire to being way ahead of the breakeven point. If you make a bet at -300, you should believe that it has at least an 85 percent chance of winning. If you make a bet at -150, then you should be thinking it has at least a 66 percent chance of winning. Anytime you are making a bet at -400 or higher, you must think that it will definitely win—90 percent is a good way to look at it.

Use the unit system when you bet the money line to maximize your winnings. As I've stressed throughout, whether your bet is a prop, a future bet, or an award bet, put more of your money where your greatest chance of victory lies.

In summary, money-line wagers are an excellent way to make money in sports gambling. It helps you eliminate the often-tough point spread. The money line allows you to pick the winner, be it the underdog or favorite. Whether you bet favorites or underdogs depends upon your personal style. Some people are better at wagering +250s than -300s. If you feel that you are good at betting underdogs, then bet mainly on those. If you feel that you are great at picking money line favorites, then stick to that.

Always turn your bet into a percentage after doing your analysis. Do you think your bet has a 60 percent chance of winning? 70 percent? 75 percent? Once you decide how much you like a bet to win in terms of a percentage, then bet the right unit amount.

2. WAGER WITH PARLAYS

Parlays are a way of making big profits without risking a lot of money. A parlay bet is one in which you bet on two or more games while only putting up one sum of money against all your games. The trick is that you have to win *all* the games you pick in order to collect on your parlay. If you bet a five-team $100 parlay and win all five, you should profit $2,000. However, if you win only four out of the five games, you lose your $100 and win nothing.

You are better off in the long run betting one game at a time rather than betting on parlays, primarily because it is tough to find four or five great bets over a couple of days. I recommend that you avoid parlays, but if you do bet a parlay on occasion, keep your bets smaller than your average straight-up bet. For example, suppose your average unit bet is $125. If you also want to bet a parlay, make it for one-third to one-half of that amount, such as $40 to $60.

Don't depend on your parlays to grow your bankroll. They're difficult to win. If you bet 5-team parlays and continually win three or four out of the five games, instead of being ahead, you'll have lost money. I may wager a parlay just two or three times a year to see what I can do. On a good day, if I am able to find three solid bets, I will wager all three straight up; but in addition, I may parlay them together for a wager. If I win all three, I am a huge winner. If I win 2 out of 3, I am still up money on the day. When I bet a parlay, I bet it with confidence, but I am never disappointed financially if it loses.

Below is a table of what your sports book should pay you in odds when betting on parlays with the spread. It also lists the real odds or chances of winning a parlay. Notice that the more games you bet, the less true payoff you get. With football parlays, if you find that the numbers dictate buying points (a concept I discuss in an upcoming section), always do so. And don't worry if your payout is less than the figures on this chart—the key is winning.

PARLAY BETS		
	Sports Book Parlay Odds	Real Odds (Chances of Winning)
2 game parlay	13/5	3 to 1
3 game parlay	6/1	7 to 1
4 game parlay	11/1	15 to 1
5 game parlay	20/1	31 to 1
6 game parlay	40/1	63 to 1
7 game parlay	75/1	127 to 1
8 game parlay	100/1	255 to 1
9 game parlay	150/1	511 to 1
10 game parlay	300/1	1,023 to 1

If your sports book is not giving you these odds, or close to them, you are not getting a fair shake and should not bet parlays with that sports book. Simply choose a different sports book for your parlay wagers.

One more point: Stay away from 6-game or bigger parlays. There are two reasons for this:

1. They do not give you very good true odds compared to the parlays of five games and under; and
2. You need a lot of luck to win a six or seven game parlay with the spread. The best approach to sports gambling is based on making good, consistent picks that are based on good information. It's hard enough to find an edge and be a winner in one game let alone six or seven games tied together.

3. HEDGE YOUR BET TO PUT MONEY IN YOUR POCKET

Hedging certain bets can often be a good move in sports gambling. Crazy things can happen to cause upsets in the four major pro sports and hedging is a way to protect against that.

Here is an example of how to take advantage of a good hedging opportunity. In 2001, the Oakland A's played the New York Yankees in a first-round, best-of-five playoff series. Because of Oakland's great pitching staff, a friend of mine really liked the A's to win the series. As I recall, the odds on their winning were +110 on the money line. He wagered $300 on Oakland to win the series, looking for a net profit of $330. Shocking the public, Oakland won the first two games in New York. The next two games were in Oakland, and all they needed was one win to move onto the next round and allow my friend to win his bet.

The betting line for the Yankees to win the series was +750 or 7 1/2 to 1 at that point. New York would have to win three straight games to win the series. My friend knew he was in a good position to win his bet, but I convinced him that anything could happen in baseball, noting that the Yankees had won three in a row before. I suggested that my friend wager $75 on the Yankees to win the series; that way, he was guaranteed a profit. If the A's hung on to win the series, he would show winnings of $330 minus the $75 he risked on New York, so he would still profit $255. If the Yankees came back to win the series, he would win $75 x 7.50 or $562.50 minus the original $300 he bet on Oakland, so he would profit $262.50. Either way, he would make a pretty good profit.

The Yankees came back to win games three and four in Oakland, and game five in New York. My friend ended up making the smart move. On the other hand, if Oakland had gone on to win the series, he wouldn't have looked bad in throwing away the extra $75 because, overall, he made a profit.

Whenever you can put yourself in a position to profit when there is significant risk the other way, it is often wise to take the money. Never look back and say, "I shouldn't have hedged my bet," because you cannot know the end result until the game is over. You hedge your bet based on the risk-versus-reward ratio.

There are many other examples of ways to hedge your bets in sports gambling. For example, you can take a team on the season to win in football. Suppose you bet the Cleveland Browns less than 6.5 games, knowing that their last game is a very hard one. If, by chance, they are 6-9 going into their last game, you can bet Cleveland on the money line to win that game at, let's say, +275. You will win either that bet, or you will win your future bet.

Now, let's say that you bet on the Dallas Mavericks to beat the Portland Trailblazers at -2 1/2 points. At halftime they have a 7-point lead. Your sports book may put out a line of Portland -1/2 a point for the second half. If so, you can look into wagering on the Trailblazers for the second half. If Dallas ends up winning by 3 to 6 points, you win both wagers. At the same time, you ensure that there is no way you can lose both bets. At worst, you go one and one.

In another example, suppose you love the Cleveland Cavaliers at home -4 points against the Denver Nuggets because Allen Iverson is injured on the Denver team, and you think Cleveland will destroy them. You are watching the game and at halftime, the Cavaliers only have a 3-point lead. At that point, if you are thinking that things don't look as good as planned, you can bet on Denver at +1 for the second half to cancel out your original bet, less a little juice that you will sacrifice. The main strategy is that, although you thought that you had a great pick to begin with, you figured that Cleveland would be up by more points at halftime, maybe 7 to 15 points. At this point, you think it might go either way, so you cancel out your original bet.

Hedging is often a good tool to use in the NFL. Suppose you bet on Pittsburgh at -5 1/2 points at home because you really expect them to smash Cleveland. At halftime, Pittsburgh is up by only 3 points. You had predicted that they would be up by at least 10 to 14 points at halftime and now think the game can go either way. At halftime, if you can get a spread on Pittsburgh at -3 points, you can bet on Cleveland at +3 to cancel out your original bet. If Pittsburgh wins by seven or more, you win your first bet, but lose your halftime bet. If Cleveland wins or loses by five or less, you win your second-half bet, but lose your original bet. Either way, at worst, you are only losing some juice by going one and one. However, if Cleveland happens to lose by exactly 6 points, you will win your original bet and push your halftime bet. You bet the second half the other way because you did not like what you were seeing, so you wanted to protect your first bet. At the same time, maybe you can profit between the two bets.

You can also hedge your bet with over/under wagers. Let say that you bet an NBA game at over 188.5 points. After the first half, your bet is looking pretty good, as the score is 55-47 for a total of 102 points. You notice that the second-half total line is set at 94.5 points. Depending on how you saw the first half go, you can take under 94 1/2 points for the second half. This way, you protect your original wager and you have the potential to win both bets. In the second half, if 86 or fewer points are scored, you will lose the first bet and win the halftime bet. In the second half, if 95 or more points are scored, you will win your original bet, but lose the halftime bet. However, if 87 to 94 points are scored in the second half, you will win both bets. The 7 points between 87 and 94 is a pretty good window, and you have a decent chance to win both bets.

Don't look back with regret if your original wager won, but your halftime one lost. You hedged your bet because things were not going well at halftime and upon reevaluating your bet, you envisioned the second half as being anybody's game.

Another example of hedging bets happens with future wagers. Let's say that during the NCAA basketball season, you think that Georgetown is an underrated, hot team. Georgetown to win the championship is at 30 to 1 odds. You then bet $30 on them, thinking they have a shot. They finish the season strong, get hot in the tournament, and make it to the NCAA finals. Now you are in a good position because you have a team that is one game away from winning money for you. However, if they lose, you will win nothing. Let's say that Georgetown is playing Georgia Tech in the finals, and Tech is a 2 1/2 point favorite and -140 on the money line. If you think the game really can go either way, the next move you make should be putting about $400 and $500 on Georgia Tech on the money line. If Tech wins, you will profit between $285 and $357 less the $30 you bet on Georgetown, for a profit between $255 and $327. If Georgetown wins, you get $900 less the $400 to $500 for a profit of $400 to $500. You made money automatically.

A friend might say, "Why hedge your bet? Go for it all!" It's because hedging allows you to take guaranteed money. This is the way you should think. Whenever you come out ahead with some decent money in your pocket, you are always a winner and never a loser.

You hedge bets to balance your risk-versus-reward ratio, to save yourself some uncertainty, or to guarantee profit. You also can hedge it to protect a percentage of your bet, say 25 percent. Every sports bet has some risk, especially when winning or losing comes down to one game. When your bet can easily go either way, 50/50 to win or lose, hedging can often be your best move. Don't be afraid to give up a little reward to eliminate your risk and put some guaranteed money in your pocket. However, if you see that your original bet is looking good, then you should stick with it.

4. TAKE ADVANTAGE OF LIVE BETTING

Many sports books are now offering "live betting," a new form of wagering that gives excellent opportunities for hedging a wager. *Live wagering* is simply betting on a game while it is being played. The sports book will offer a line on the match that takes into account two main factors: the original spread in the game, and the current score. With live betting, you have the option of hedging your bet at the time in the game that is most favorable for you. You can use live betting as a tool to protect some of the big wagers that you make. It is a great asset to have when you make a good or great bet. If your team isn't winning easily, you should be in a position during most of the game where you can bet the other way to take away some of your risk.

For example, suppose you have bet on the Lakers at home -2 points against the San Antonio Spurs. With 9 minutes left in the fourth quarter, the Lakers have a minute 1-point lead. You really think the game can go either way, so you decide you want to get out of your original bet. If your sports book offers a line of San Antonio at +2, you can wager on San Antonio and cancel out your original bet. If you can get San Antonio at +2 1/2 or +3 or +1 1/2, you can still hedge your bet, since you are not going to lose both bets with the new hedge wager. In this situation, hedging may be a smart move as it looks to be anyone's game. By hedging, you can take back your original money minus some juice, and start looking for your next good or great wager.

In addition to hedging, live betting can offer some good wagering opportunities. If you can pick up on a key factor in a game—possibly a key player is injured, maybe one team looks totally flat and the other looks very impressive, maybe there is a matchup in the game that you really like, or perhaps you think that the original spread is way off base—then you may have a good betting opportunity.

You can also bet on a team that has momentum. Suppose a team that is down by big points in the fourth quarter makes a run and sends the game into overtime. With all the positive momentum, the team that fought back usually will win in overtime as the other team is mentally down.

For the most part, live betting is a good tool for betting on quality underdog teams. Often, an underdog team can take a decent lead in a match, be it basketball, football or baseball. The thing with live betting is that the spread is designed assuming that the favorite is going to make a big run at some time during the game. Often they do, but often they don't. You have to find the games where you think the favorite will not complete a comeback. If you see no reason why the underdog cannot hang onto the lead, and if you believe the underdog is a quality team, then you can bet on the underdog and take the points you currently have.

In the NBA playoffs I once wagered on the New Jersey Nets at -220 to win the match while having an 18-point, second-quarter lead in Miami. I could have wagered on the point spread at -6 and -120, but I opted for the money line. The spread stood at only -6 and -220 on the money line for New Jersey because the original spread had Miami favored by 5 points. Watching the game, I saw no reason why New Jersey couldn't hang on and win the game; after all, they also were an NBA playoff team. Miami managed to make a small run, but the 18-point lead was too big and New Jersey won the game by a solid margin.

If Miami had had an 18-point lead in the second quarter, the line on Miami to win the match would have been -1600 or so, and a point spread of -14—no value there, nothing to bet on. Betting on the favorite in live betting only works when you think your favorite is going to decisively beat the other team.

Overall, be very careful with live betting. It is hard to win in the long run making quick financial decisions with a lot of risk and uncertainty involved. Be careful and only make live wagers when a bet really stands out.

5. MAKE HALFTIME BETS

Most good sports books will offer you halftime wagers with an over/under line and a spread line, as well as a money line for the half. Some sports books will even offer you a line on how many points each individual team will score in the second half. The two primary sports for this are football and basketball.

What advantage does the educated sports gambler have with halftime bets? Your primary advantage is that, if the game is being broadcast, you can see how the game is playing out.

The halftime spread is always connected to the original line in the game and is also based on the results of the first half. If by watching the first half you see the original line was way off, you may find a good bet to take advantage of. Usually, the more Team A is losing by, the more a favorite they will be in the second half. Teams that are ahead usually will be less aggressive in the second half, while teams that are down will play as aggressively as possible to give themselves a chance to come back.

These are the seven main things you should look for in halftime spreads.

1. How is the flow of the game going? Compared to the original spread in the game, does it look like more of an over or more of an under?
2. How is the weather affecting the game?
3. Is one team totally dominating the other team, or is the score misleading? Is one team overachieving, or is another team underachieving?
4. Does the team that is losing appear to be poised to make a run in the second half? Or is the team outmatched and probably will be outscored again in the second half?

5. Is there one matchup in the game that is destroying one team, thus affecting whether the game will go over or under? For example, the Dallas Cowboys cannot run against Washington's run defense; or the Dallas Mavericks have no chance at stopping the Phoenix Suns' offense, as it's either an Amare dunk or a Nash lay-up consistently down the floor.

6. Were there any injuries or ejections to key players that will have a significant outcome on the second half of the game?

7. What adjustments do you foresee the teams making for the second half?

You can use halftime bets as tools to protect the original bets you made on the game. As I wrote in the section on hedging, there are many ways to accomplish this. Let's say that you bet on the Milwaukee Bucks -1 at home against the Lakers. You risked $330 to win $300, because you knew that Lamar Odom would not be playing for the Lakers and you felt that Milwaukee was a solid bet. You are now watching the first half and see that Odom's loss is not as big a factor as you thought. Kobe Bryant is having a great game, and the Bucks are looking decent at best. At halftime, the Bucks have a 3-point lead, which is so small it's almost meaningless. You notice that the line for the second half is a pick. You are not so confident in your original bet at this point, so you decide to hedge your bet by betting on the Lakers in the second half. You have the potential to protect your original bet, and possibly win both bets.

L.AKERS VS. BUCKS SAMPLE SECOND HALF BET
- Betting On L.A. Second Half at a Pick, (No Spread)
- Milwaukee is up at the half 49-46.
- Original Wager on Milwaukee -1 for the game

Final Game Result	Wagers Result
a) If Lakers win game	Lose original, win halftime
b) If Milwaukee wins game by 4 or more	Win original, lose halftime
c) If Milwaukee wins by 3	Win original, push halftime
d) If Milwaukee wins by 2	Win original, win halftime
e) If Milwaukee wins by 1	Push original, win halftime

Looking at the five potential outcomes for the game, you are in great position. You have protected your original bet with the potential to win both, or maybe push one and win the other. If you bet a full $330 to win $300 on the Lakers in the second half, the most you can lose is $30, but you have the potential to win both bets for $600.

It would be less likely for the Bucks to win by exactly 1 to 3 points, but you are not as confident in Milwaukee as you first thought after watching the first half, and you want to diminish your risk. Remember, you don't have to hedge your entire first bet. You can cut your bet in half by wagering $165 on the Lakers' second half. Bet only as much at halftime as makes sense in order to protect your bet. On the other hand, if the Bucks are up by nine at halftime and the spread is Lakers at -3 1/2 for the second half, you can let your bet ride with the 9-point lead. You don't need to hedge it, although you can hedge it in the hope that the Bucks win by one to 5 points.

MORE ON HALFTIME WAGERS

NBA halftime scores are often meaningless. Great teams can be down at home by 7 points or more and come back to win the game. With the 24-second shot clock ticking, it is easy to come back in the NBA.

If your original bet is losing at halftime, depending on the spreads and situation, you will not be able to hedge your bet at the half. You will just have to stick with your original wager and hope it makes a comeback. In the Lakers/Bucks example, if the Lakers have a 7-point lead at the half, then all you can do is hope that Milwaukee comes back and wins the game for your original bet. You can't wager on the Lakers for the second half at, let's say, +1. If you do and they win the game by 1 to 5 points, you lose both bets.

Hedging also works in the NFL, because you can often put yourself in a position to win both bets. In the NFL, a halftime score is more meaningful than it is in the NBA. Unlike the NBA, which is a game of runs, the NFL is a game of moving the ball and big plays that lead to scoring points.

Remember that you can only hedge your bet at halftime if your wager is winning or is almost tied, and you are able to secure a second-half wager that correlates with your original wager. The only reason to hedge your bet is to reduce risk; otherwise you let it ride. For example, if you bet $440 to win $400 on the Colts -7 at home against KC, and the Colts are up by 17 at the half, you do not have to hedge your bet if the line is KC -3 at the half. You can let it ride because you are in a good position. However, you can do a slight hedge and take KC for the second half, risking $110 to win $100 to protect your original bet by $100. If KC loses by 8 to 13 points, you win both bets.

One other key point to know about halftime bets is that you often will see that the over/under for the second half is exactly one-half of what the original total was. If you see a high-scoring first half in basketball and all signs look to another high-scoring half, you might want to bet the second half over. Let's say that two teams combined for 107 points in the first half, and the second half over/under is only 90 1/2. Based on the tempo of the game, if you see no reason why they cannot easily score over 90 1/2, you may have a good wager at hand. Often, the tempo of the game can be a lot faster then Vegas anticipated.

Or suppose you witness a shootout in the first half of a football game. You can analyze whether the first half will repeat itself or it was simply an aberration. I recall a game between the Toronto Raptors and Detroit Pistons in which Ben Wallace got ejected in the first half. The first half was high scoring and the line was low for the second half. With Ben, the best defensive player, out of the game I knew it would help the over a great deal. I ended up cruising to victory by wagering on the over for the second half.

Be very careful not to bet games under in the second half, especially in the NBA or college basketball. Because of late game fouling and overtime, it is never a safe bet to bet a basketball game under in the second half. Look to bet the over or don't bet it at all. Only bet a second half under if you find a great spread that really stands out, or you are hedging your original bet.

Anything can happen in sports—and the potential for trouble is doubly true with halftime bets. In one-half of a game, the chances for a lesser team outplaying a better team are even greater. In 2008, suppose the Boston Celtics, a great defensive team, play the Philadelphia 76ers, an average offensive team. It would be tough for Philadelphia to score 110 points; however, it would not be a shocker if they had one great half and scored 55 points.

A halftime bet can be a good way to make money. It is also a key tool in hedging and protecting your original bets when there is reasonable doubt and risk involved.

6. BET ON AWARDS

I have seen some crazy finishes that have cost me a lot of money, and I've seen a lot of crazy finishes that have made money for me as well. That is one reason why, in addition to the regular wagers that I make, I take advantage of different sports wagering opportunities that have more certainty. One of those opportunities is betting on awards.

It isn't too hard to predict who will win MVP or Rookie of the Year awards towards the end of the season. There are few upsets at that point. The voters generally vote for the most deserving candidate. By analyzing the statistics of past winners, you can often accurately predict the eventual winner.

For example, in early August 2003, my sports book put out odds on who would win the American League Cy Young Award. The main candidates were Esteban Loaiza, Andy Petite, Roy Halladay and Mark Mulder. The odds were 3 to 1 on Halladay and 2 to 1 on Loaiza. Pedro Martinez was a long shot because he had been injured all year. There were some other pitchers listed who had little or no chance to win it. Then I heard that Mark Mulder was going to be out for the season with an elbow injury. I broke down the wager by making a chart with the key stats of every pitcher in the AL who was having a good year. I discovered that, with only eight games left for each pitcher to start, there were only two real candidates: Loaiza, who was second in E.R.A., and Halladay, who was first in wins. I wagered on both of them, knowing that I would show a profit if either of them won. Halladay won by a landslide and Loaiza finished second.

I also remember betting on Anquan Boldin to win NFL rookie of the year at odds of 5 to 1. At the time he had about 45 catches through eight games, and was on pace to break the rookie record for receptions in a season, which he did. I got a line of +500 on the favorite. What a line!

A key thing to remember when betting on awards is that the MVP award is based not only on stats, but team performance as well. The MVP award is not usually given to the best player, but the most valuable player on his team. It is almost impossible to win MVP in any league unless your team had a remarkable season and finished as a top-five team in the league. Coach of the Year is also directly linked to team success.

However, rookie of the year and most other awards usually are based on pure season statistics with little or no link to a team's success in the season. When wagering on any award, search and check to find out the names of the award winners for the past five years. What were each award winner's stats? What was his team's success story for that season? Also look at the stats of the players who finished in second, third and fourth place. Factor these stats into your wager and compare the statistics of the frontrunners for the award this season.

When betting on awards, it is usually a safe move to wager on two players when possible and financially feasible. If one player gets seriously injured during the season, you have the second player as a backup. Here's another good tip when betting awards: If you see that someone else has taken over as the favorite to win the award several weeks or months into the season, you can hedge your bet with the new favorite if you can still get a line on the wager.

When making these bets, check out as many articles as possible on the award to gather the sports writers' opinions. This information is important because the sports writers usually are the ones voting on the awards!

Award betting can be a solid way to make money with sports handicapping. Don't worry about having to wait until the season is over for your wager to be graded. You should always make a good or great bet when you find it. Don't bet on awards before the season starts because too many things can happen. It is usually better to wait and see what each player's stats are for at least 25 percent of the season before betting, and preferably 50-75 percent through a league schedule. The closer you are to the end of the season, the more secure an award bet you can find.

7. BUY POINTS

Buying points is a way in which you can move a few points off the spread in your favor. However, doing so changes the money line on your wager, and you end up risking more money than the usual -110. Usually the money line will move about 10 percent for every 1/2 point you buy. For example, suppose the Washington Redskins are playing in New York against the Jets and the spread is Washington +2 1/2. You like the Redskins to win or keep it close with their decent defense, but you want to move the spread to Washington at +3 1/2. In that case, the money line might move from -110 to -130 or -140.

Is buying points a good move? It can be depending on the sport, spread and game. Football, and especially the NFL, is the sport in which buying points means the most. You certainly can get good value by doing so. The key numbers in the NFL are 3, 4 and 7, the numbers by which games are most often won. In fact, NFL games are so often won by 3 points that 3 is the most important number in buying points.

FOOTBALL

In the 2004 NFL season, 256 games were played, 47 of which were decided by exactly 3 points! That works out to 18.36 percent, or almost one out of every five games. Just by looking at the teams, you know that a few games every week are going to be blowouts. If you remove those games, you'd expect about one game in four to be decided by 3 points. If a game goes into overtime, chances are good that it will be decided by a field goal—and there's your 3 points right there. Your key is deciding when and where buying points will give you an advantage with the spread.

The best thing to do with a 3-point spread is simple: If you analyzed the game and love the underdog, buy 1/2 a point and take the underdog to +3 1/2. If you like the favorite a lot, do the opposite: Buy 1/2 a point and take it down to -2 1/2. In both cases, if the game is decided by a field goal—and there is a decent chance it will be because the spread is 3—you are in good position to win.

The next-best way to buy points is with 7-point spreads. Buying it down to -6 1/2 with the favorite is good, while taking it up to +7 1/2 with the underdog is also good. This way, you win if the game is decided by 7 points. You are simply making your favorite have to win by only one score for you to make money, while your underdog can lose by one score and you win.

Buying points in the NFL is better than buying them in college football, because college kickers often miss extra points, the overtime format is different, and there is a lot more parity in the NFL.

Except for the situations described above, I don't recommend buying points in other NFL situations. Moving a spread of 6 down to 2 1/2 is not good because you will end up risking too much money. It will cost you a line of -180 or more to get a line down to -2.5. It's not worth it because you would be risking $180 to win $100. If you like the bet to win, either take it at -6 or don't take it at all.

I advise against buying points on over/unders in football because it is hard to determine if buying that extra point has value. Some pros put a good value on 35, 38 and 42 because a lot of games are in that range: 20-17, 21-14, and 24-17 are final scores that come up quite often. Just do the smart thing by getting a good spread at the right time.

COLLEGE AND NBA BASKETBALL
In both college and NBA basketball, bet strictly with the spread or the money line, nothing in-between. It's not worth it because one or 2 points don't matter much in a basketball game. You should not be putting up more than the -110 in a basketball spread wager. Either take the team with the spread or on the money line.

You are already risking juice with -110.

BASEBALL
In baseball, I generally do not recommend buying a run because one run in a baseball game is not much. You are better off just taking a team with the regular money line. You usually can get good money lines on good teams with hot pitchers. However, there are some unique times when I think it can be wise to wager on a baseball team at -1 1/2.

Here are some guidelines to follow when betting a baseball club at -1 1/2:

Your best bet is taking road teams at -1 1/2 because you are assured that your team will get all nine innings to bat. Suppose you take a home team at -1 1/2 and they are up one run. If they shut down their opponent in the top of the ninth, your home team will not bat in the bottom of the inning, and will not be able cover the spread. Extra innings are another reason it is wiser to take only road teams at -1 1/2. If you take a home team at -1.5, you are putting your bet at a disadvantage, because the only way you can win is with a home run.

Only pick your home team at -1 1/2 when you believe that two things are in place:

a. You have picked the more dominant team
b. You have picked the better pitcher.

Asking a better team in baseball to win by two runs is not too much to ask for and you can move a line of -250 or -220 down to -140 or so at -1 1/2, not a bad thing if you pick the right game.

HOCKEY
Finally, I do not recommend buying goals in hockey. You might think that taking a team at +1 1/2 is a good idea in a potentially low-scoring hockey game. But the main problem is that your team can be down a goal late, then give up an empty net score and lose by two. Taking a team at -1 1/2 in hockey is not a good bet because it is tough to ask your team to win by two goals in any hockey game, and you cannot rely on the empty-net goal to help you win. Overall, hockey is probably the toughest of all four sports to wager. Buying a goal or selling a goal just makes things tougher. When wagering on hockey, I recommend taking teams with the money line or -.5 or +.5, not at +1 1/2 or -1 1/2.

SUMMARY

Buying points is an effective sports gambling tool, but you must pick your spots in the right games with the right spreads. Don't listen to handicappers who tell you never to buy points. It can be a very effective tool while wagering in the NFL, especially moving lines from -3 to -2 1/2 or +3 to +3 1/2. Again, it all comes down to your risk-versus-reward ratio.

10

5 MORE WAYS TO WIN

1. PLACE PROPOSITION BETS ON INDIVIDUAL PLAYERS

In proposition bets, you are betting on the performance of one or two individual players rather than the performance of an entire team. Your sports book often sets the line on prop bets, whereas Las Vegas sets the line for regular game wagers. Thus, you can find more inequalities with the prop lines.

When betting on proposition bets, stick to basketball and football. I don't like hockey and baseball prop bets because of the inconsistent results of the players. In these sports, anyone can step up and play well in a game, while great players can do nothing. For example, let's say that you bet on Alex Rodriguez over 1.5 hits. You know you are betting on one of the best players in baseball, but he can just as easily go 0-3, 1-4, or 2-4 on that day. On the same day an average player may go 3-4 with one home run and 6 RBIs. Pat Borders, a mediocre hitter for the Toronto Blue Jays during the season, won the World Series MVP in the early 90s because he played a great six games. There is usually no pattern to help guide your wager.

You can pick up on patterns in basketball and football. In the NBA finals, you never see players such as Malik Rose or Devean George win the MVP, because each player in basketball is assigned his role on the team, and is set with a certain amount of minutes a game and about the same number of shots per game.

You can make two types of proposition bets: an individual player's stats and a matchup bet. First, let's look at making an individual player's performance bet. In basketball, the bet can be on how many points Yao Ming will score or how many rebounds he will take down. You can bet on stats like the number of assists, blocked shots, minutes played. In football, it can be stats like the number of passing yards, receiving yards, rushing yards, or sacks.

All your prop bets should have logic to them. You should avoid prop bets that are based on pure luck, because in the long run, you will not win with them. For example, bets such as: Who will score first? Who will nail a coffin corner punt first? Will the coin toss be heads or tails? Who will score the first 10 points of the game? Will the teams' total be odd or even? These are examples of pure anything-can-happen types of bets. You may win on one day, but you are betting for the long term. If you are going to bet props like that, you might as well take your money to the roulette tables and try your luck there by betting on black or red.

The real question is, "How can you figure out how many points or rebounds a player will get?" The first thing you need to do is analyze the line based on the player's past performance. Go to the league's website and click the player's stats to see what he averages for the year. More importantly, click on game log or game-by-game results to see his last five or 10 games. Also check to see how he did against the current opposing team the last time they met. The line the sports books gives you usually will be about the average that a player gets for the season.

Let's say that Allen Iverson averages 26 points per game in the regular season. The line you get will be somewhere between 25 and 27 points. Now, how can you decide if you have a good pick? First, you have to look at his last five games. Is he getting a lot of shots? Is he getting a lot of playing time?

You are looking for two main variables that will determine whether you take Allen Iverson over, under, or not take the prop at all.

1) **Is he playing a defensive, slow-it-down team? Or is he playing an offensive, run-and-gun team? Who is covering him? How did he do the last time he played this team?**

Although what happened in the last meeting is a factor, don't put too much weight on it. There is a much better chance of his going over against an offensive team that plays little defense (like the Golden State Warriors in 2007/2008), because he will get a lot more shots and more possessions. You also must consider whether Iverson is going against a great defensive player such as Bruce Bowen or Tayshaun Prince.

Here is an example of an NBA game in which a great player went up against a defensive star. In Carmelo Anthony's rookie year, he averaged an impressive 21-plus points per game as he carried his team to a big turnaround and to the playoffs. Very early in the season, Anthony was on the road playing the Indiana Pacers. The line on him was 17 points. I would almost never bet a player such as Anthony under because he is such an explosive scorer. I liked betting him over when the right time came, but this was not the right time. I didn't think it was a good pick because he was playing against the best perimeter defender in the league, Ron Artest (who went on to win defensive player of the year award that season), and the Indiana Pacers were one of the top seven defensive teams in the NBA. Indiana and Artest ended up holding him to his season low of 2 points!

Things can go both ways. At times, you will find that a player goes up against a great defensive player/team and scores a lot of points. But, for the most part, your bet should be partially based on who your player is playing, and then look to bet over or under in combination with the other factors.

Upon the completion of the 2005 NBA Eastern Conference Finals, Tayshaun Prince was averaging 14.7 points per game in the playoffs. However, in the finals, he played against a great defensive team in San Antonio. The prop line on him in every game in the finals was either 13 or 14 points. Here are his stats for the seven games: Game 1, 11 points; Game 2, 3 points; Game 3, 12 points; Game 4, 13 points; Game 5, 10 points; Game 6, 13 points; Game 7, 9 points.

If you had bet Prince under every game in the NBA finals, you would have won or pushed every bet. The low-scoring games were not a coincidence—he was playing against the best defensive team in the league. If Prince had played against the Phoenix Suns in the finals, I believe he would have scored over 13 points at least a couple of times.

2) On Iverson's team, who is injured or is not playing because of other reasons?

For example, suppose Allen Iverson is the leading scorer for the Denver Nuggets at 26 points per game. He has two teammates who are secondary scorers, Carmelo Anthony at 25 points per game and Kenyon Martin at 13 points per game. If Martin or Anthony is injured, then Iverson can be a very good bet to go over because, instead of Iverson passing the ball around and only taking his usual 19 shots per game, he might carry more of the team's offensive load. He will probably end up taking 25 to 30 shots, because somebody has to shoot the ball more often, and it usually ends up being the team's best scorer.

Here is an example of a situation where I took advantage of an injury. In the late 1990s, the Detroit Pistons were playing the Miami Heat in the first round of the playoffs and were losing the series two games to zero in a best-of-five. In game two, Grant Hill had a badly injured foot and everyone knew that he would not play in game three. The Detroit Pistons were basically a two-man team offensively—the ball either went through Hill's hands or Jerry Stackhouse's hands—so I knew that Stackhouse would be taking a lot more shots in a must-win game. Stackhouse was a great scorer at the time and I figured that, with Hill out, he would step up his offensive game. The line came out on Stackhouse at 17 1/2 points.

I jumped on the bet, taking the over at 17 1/2 and -135. I knew that Stackhouse would be taking a lot of shots and I also liked the fact that he went to the foul line a lot. This is important because a great shooter can go cold from the field and not get his points. But a player who drives the ball to the basket and goes to the foul line is a more reliable scorer than a player who gets most of his points from outside jump shots. The betting line closed at 18 points and -200 on the over; other bettors knew it was a great bet, as well. I thought that the only way I could lose was if he got injured. What happened? Stackhouse took 21 shots and 13 free throw attempts as he finished the game with 25 points in a Piston loss. The bet very easily covered the line.

During the Shaq and Kobe era with the Los Angeles Lakers, whenever Shaq was injured, Kobe would often have monster scoring games. In the streak that Kobe had—ten straight 40-point games—Shaq missed about half of those games.

The opposite is also true: If a key player is coming back from injury, someone else on the team should end up with fewer minutes and shots.

Here is another good tip: Some big men play well and put up big numbers against teams that have no true center. Zydrunas Ilgauskas always puts up big numbers against teams with no strong defensive center, but he often does little against teams that have a good one.

It is better to wager a player at over 19 1/2 points in a game with a total of 210 points than in a game with a total of 185 points, and vice versa.

For example, let's say that the Cleveland Cavaliers are hosting the Charlotte Bobcats. Cleveland is favored by 11 points and the total for the game is only 178 points. If you are thinking of taking Lebron James at over 30 1/2 points, that is probably a bad bet because of the low total in the game. Also, there is a good chance that Cleveland will be up by 15 to 20 points in the fourth quarter, with James sitting on the bench instead of being on the court where you need him to be scoring points. Always remember that it is more likely that a superstar will get more points during a close game, because the team will feed the ball to the go-to guy and give him more scoring opportunities. In a blowout, the stars are either on the bench or are just having fun getting everyone involved by passing.

As a perfect example, Michael Jordan had his big 50-point games during close games where his team was expecting him to win the game for them. When the Bulls won by big points, he usually would only score between 20 and 30 points. No player would want to embarrass another team with a 50-point outing when they are up by 20 points.

MATCHUP PROPS

Basketball or football matchup props are similar to individual props. In both props, you are betting on a player's individual stats for one game. The main difference is that two players' stats are involved in matchup props. You can find a line of who will get more points, Allen Iverson at -5 1/2 points -110 to Kevin Durant, or Shaq at +1 1/2 -120 rebounds to Tim Duncan. Or in football, you can find Larry Johnson at -8 1/2 rushing yards versus LaDainian Tomlinson.

In matchup bets, instead of looking for an edge in one player's stats, you have to look at two players' game stats, and that makes things a lot harder. Overall, I recommend being careful with matchup bets and making limited wagers on bets you really like a lot because so many things are up in the air. You may love Allen Iverson to have a great game against a weak Seattle defense and he might play great and score 37 points, but at the same time, you have to worry about Kevin Durant, who may go off for 33 points the same night and cover the 5 1/2 point spread. In the long run, you are much better off just taking the individual prop. Your main player might do what you forecast, while the other man either plays miserably or plays too well and ruins your bet.

The key with matchup bets is getting an advantage with minutes or shots or rushing attempts or whatever prop it is. I once took Kobe Bryant at -2 1/2 points against Shareef Abdur-Rahim. The reason I liked it so much was because Rahim had just been traded to Portland, and on his new team, he would be coming off the bench. Anytime you can take a great scorer such as Kobe Bryant against a guy coming off the bench, you have a great bet. Bench players have a short time to prove their worth on the court. If they play really well, they may be given fourth-quarter minutes; if they don't play well, they usually will be relegated to the bench and not get those key extra minutes needed to score points.

Since matchup props are tough to beat, I only recommend them when something really stands out. The fewer variables in any gambling scenario, the less the chance that something will go wrong. The more variables, the greater the chance that your bet will lose. That is a key point to remember.

FOOTBALL PROPS
In football, the best prop bets are quarterback attempts, quarterback completions, quarterback passing yards, running back rushing yards, wide receiver receiving yards, wide receiver catches, and running back attempts.

You might ask, "How am I supposed to guess how many yards a certain player will be getting in an individual match?"

In a football game, quite often the losing quarterback ends up with more passing yards than the winning quarterback. This is because the team that is behind is forced to keep throwing the football in order to save time and find a way to get back into the game. When a team is down, they often entirely abandon the running game and just pass, pass, pass. You will sometimes find that a quarterback has thrown for over 400 yards but his team has lost the game. For example, in the 2004 NFL season, Jake Plummer threw for 499 yards but his team lost 41-28.

If you find an average quarterback playing a great team that has a high-powered offense, take the average quarterback over in passing yards if you like the bet. I suggest the over because his team will be constantly trying to match the other team's points with scores, and even if he doesn't score, it might not matter. You might win because of the yardage he racks up trying to score.

For example, during the 2004 NFL season, Baltimore played the Philadelphia Eagles in Philly. At the time, the Eagles were playing great football and were undefeated. Philly was favored by 7 1/2 points in the game. Kyle Boller was the quarterback for Baltimore. He didn't throw for many yards during the season because Baltimore usually ran the ball with Jamal Lewis, the best running back in the league at the time. During the previous season, Lewis topped 2,000 rushing yards. The line on Boller was 170 1/2 yards. Not only was it a low line, the over was at +170. In the first six games of the season, Boller, an average quarterback, had averaged only 123 yards passing per game.

The typical bettor would have looked at that and thought, "He has only averaged 123 yards so far, and now he is up against one of the best defenses in football, so he will get few passing yards." Anyone betting the under made a bad wager for two main reasons. First of all, never take any quarterback in the NFL under 170 1/2 yards, because a bet like that leaves you no room for error. A couple of big plays and you lose. Any quarterback starting in the NFL is a decent quarterback or he wouldn't be there. Further, any starting quarterback can throw for over 170 1/2 yards on any given Sunday.

The second and most important reason that bettors picked wrong in taking the under is that Philadelphia would likely be winning the game most of the way; they were big favorites. If the game went its course, Baltimore would have to increase their passing downs and decrease their rushing attempts in order to get back into the game. I would have made that bet at -110; +170 was great. What happened? Philly had the lead the entire way, and Baltimore started passing a lot more. Philly ended up winning the game, but the Ravens kept pushing back and Boller kept passing, finishing with 223 passing yards, going over 170 1/2 yards fairly easily.

Following is a list of what to look for in terms of positions and yards. Remember you have to like the pick to begin with.

QB PASSING YARDS/OVER

- Playing against a great offense
- QB is a capable proven past performer
- Playing in a dome or clear weather
- Playing against a weak defense
- A game in which you think your player's team will be trailing most of game

QB PASSING YARDS/UNDER

- Playing against a weak offense
- A poor or average quarterback
- A game in which you think your player's team will be ahead most of the game
- Poor weather conditions, including either snow, rain, a slippery field, or strong winds
- Playing against good secondary and/or pass rush

QB ATTEMPTS/OVER

- Playing against a great offense
- A game in which you think your player's team will be trailing most of the game
- A QB whose team likes to abandon the run
- A QB whose team likes to throw in short yardage situations

QB ATTEMPTS/UNDER

- Playing against a weak offense
- A game in which you think your QB's team will be ahead most of the game
- A QB whose team likes to run a lot
- A QB whose team likes to run in short yardage situations

QB COMPLETIONS/OVER

- QB is a capable and proven performer
- Playing in a dome or clear weather during game
- A game in which you think your player's team will be trailing most of the game
- Playing against a great offense
- A QB whose team likes to throw in short yardage situations

QB COMPLETIONS/UNDER

- An inconsistent quarterback with his throws
- Poor weather conditions, including snow/rain/slippery field/very windy
- A game in which you think your player's team will be ahead most of the game
- Playing against a weak offense
- A QB whose team likes to run in short yardage situations

WIDE RECEIVER RECEPTIONS/OVER
- A proven consistent receiver
- A game in which you think your player's team will be trailing most of the game
- A receiver that has a very capable, consistent quarterback
- Playing against a great offense
- A team that makes a lot of short passes, and likes to throw in short yardage
- Playing in a dome or in clear weather

WIDE RECEIVER RECEPTIONS/UNDER
- An erratic receiver, inconsistent receiver
- A non-starter
- A receiver who has a poor or average quarterback
- A receiver who is not a main target of the quarterback
- A receiver who is on a team that loves to run
- A game in which you think your player's team will be ahead most of the game
- Poor weather conditions including either snow/rain/ slippery field/very windy

WIDE RECEIVER RECEIVING YARDS/OVER
- A deep threat, a big-play receiver who is capable of one, two or three plus-25-yard catches
- A proven, consistent receiver
- A game in which you think your player's team will be trailing most of the game
- A receiver that has a very capable, consistent quarterback
- Playing against a great offense

WIDE RECEIVER RECEIVING YARDS/UNDER

- A possession receiver who rarely makes a big yardage catch
- An erratic or inconsistent receiver
- A non-starter
- A receiver who is on a team that loves to run
- A game in which you think your player's team will be ahead most of the game

RUNNING BACK CARRIES/OVER

- A consistent running back who has proven he can move the chains
- A game in which you think your player's team will be ahead most of the game
- Playing against a weak rushing defense
- Playing against a weak offense
- A running back that gets consistent carries each week
- A team that loves to run in short yardage

RUNNING BACK CARRIES/UNDER

- A game in which you think your player's team will be trailing most of the game
- A running back who is inconsistent in his performance
- Playing against a great rushing defense
- A team that likes to pass a lot and abandon the run
- A team that loves to pass in short yardage
- A non-starter

RUNNING BACK YARDS/OVER

- A consistent running back who has proven he can make plays
- A RB who has proven he can break for a 15-plus-yard carry twice or more a game

- A game in which you think your player's team will be ahead most of the game
- A RB whose team will not abandon the run and will get consistent carries
- Playing against a weak rushing defense
- A team that loves to run in short yardage

RUNNING BACK YARDS/UNDER

- A game in which you think your player's team will be trailing most of the game
- A running back that has shown he cannot make big plays very often
- Playing against a strong rushing defense
- A team that likes to pass a lot and abandon the run
- A non-starter
- A running back that does not get consistent carries

I did not discuss the stats for the player you are betting on because the line you get will probably be the average that he has had all season. When betting on receivers, tight ends, and running backs under in yards, be cautious with the amount you bet because one play can beat you at any time.

Be aware that if a backup running back, tight end or wide receiver is starting because the regular starter has been injured, the backup's stats will rise dramatically. If you can get a low spread on a backup who is starting, look to bet the over. If you believe that he will get a lot of carries or passes thrown his way, he should go over the low spread easily. A lot of the time, the backup will come in and have very similar stats to what the starter had. Any NFL running back can run with a good offensive line. And any NFL receiver or tight end can catch the ball with a good quarterback and good passing game. Look to take advantage in these situations.

Use the spread as a guide when you consider whether your prop player's team will be trailing or ahead in the game. This is very important for the point I made earlier: When a team is down, especially in the second half, it will be passing more. When they are ahead, they will be running more. Basic football stuff, but a major factor in your prop bet.

When trying to determine whether a team has a good or poor rushing defense, just check the rankings on the Internet. Do not look at passing defense stats as much because these stats are not as reliable. They are based on how a team's games go with their offense and are not a true measure. As a rule, when measuring a team's defense, look more at points allowed than yardage allowed. Points are a much more credible stat because any team that has a lead is going to give up yardage, as the other team will be primarily passing on each play.

Props can be an excellent way to make money, but don't bet on a prop just because you think the line is off by a point or two. Bet on it because you think there is a significant chance of the prop bet going your way, whether over or under. There are so many lines to choose from that if you stay disciplined with your props in basketball and football and only bet when you feel you have a good edge, you can make money.

SEASON BETS

I often like to bet on season-long bets because I am putting money on the results of a whole season, not on one game where the worst team in the league can beat the best team. Over an 82-game season in the NBA or NHL, or 162 games in MLB, the true stats will win out. Whenever you can find prop bets based on the entire season, see if you can get an advantage.

In the 2003-2004 NBA season, I bet Carmelo Anthony at +8 1/2 points to Kevin Garnett on the regular season points the two players would average head-to-head. I loved the bet because I knew Carmelo would be playing in Denver, a team that had little talent, and that he would be the number-one scoring option. I knew Carmelo averaged over 22 points a game in the Big East, so I figured that he would get at least 16 in the NBA. It was a good bet: Carmelo averaged over 21 points per game and I won my wager.

When making long-term season bets with teams, it is more secure to bet on teams under rather than over. Why? Because of the injury bug. The spread is made assuming that the team will be relatively healthy all year. Any team can have bad luck with injuries and just fall apart, no matter how good they may look in the preseason or on paper. Remember the Spurs in the 1996-1997 season? They were projected to win about 50 games, but their team got hit by major injuries and they went on to win only 20 out of 82 games. I am not saying that you should never bet a team over in a long season bet—if you love it, take it. But remember that injuries can hurt your wager. The great thing about betting unders with season bets is that all injuries help you. For example, if a key basketball player is injured for only three weeks, his team may go 3-7 in the 10 games he misses, turning your bet into a winner.

Also, look to bet unders on young teams. If the talent is the same, experience is the next biggest factor to a team's success. Experienced teams or players do the little things that help a team win, while younger players often make mistakes that help a team lose.

In summary, when you bet big on season wagers, be careful with NFL season bets, because with only 16 games played, even a mediocre team can fluke off a couple of close games and finish the season at 9-7. In the other three major sports, you cannot hide from an 82- or 162-game season.

2. FIND WINDOWS OF OPPORTUNITY BY MIDDLING

A great middling situation became available during the 2003 NHL Stanley Cup Playoffs. Going into the finals, New Jersey was to face Anaheim, a number-seven seed. But Anaheim was on fire as an underdog, and had eliminated top teams Dallas and Detroit with ease. However, at the start of the NHL finals, New Jersey was still a favorite at -165 to win the series. My sports book also posted odds for NHL Playoffs MVP.

The NHL is different from basketball, baseball and football in that they award the MVP on the entire playoffs, not just the finals. Jean-Sebastien Giguere, Anaheim's goalie, had been dominating the NHL playoffs, saving almost every shot that came his way. In one series, he gave up only one goal in four games with unprecedented, spectacular play.

The odds on Giguere were posted at 2 to 1. I knew that if Anaheim won the Cup, Giguere was, barring injury, very likely to win the MVP. Even if he missed most of the finals due to injury, he still most likely would win. Also, if New Jersey won, he still had a shot at MVP. I checked on the Internet and found that four times previously in Stanley Cup Playoffs history, the MVP went to a player on the losing team. So, I balanced my wager and bet on both New Jersey to win the series at -165 and Giguere to win MVP at +200. I set it up so that, even if I only won one of the wagers, I would still have a very small profit. I could do that because the +200 that I was getting was stronger than the -165 I was giving up. (If my odds had been +150 and

-165, I still would have made the wager, since even if I had lost one, I would have only lost a little juice.)

My possible outcomes were:

1. Anaheim wins the Cup, I would lose the series, and Giguere wins MVP. I win one bet, lose one bet
2. New Jersey wins the Cup, I would win the series, and Giguere loses MVP. I win one bet, lose one bet
3. New Jersey wins the Cup, I would win the series, and Giguere wins MVP. I win both bets!

The end result was outcome number three. New Jersey won the Cup in seven tightly contested games, and the only contenders for MVP were Martin Brodeur and Giguere, who won it. I was in a no-lose situation. Fortunately, things worked out so that I won both bets.

Here is a list of the different types of bets where you can find middling opportunities.

TYPES OF WINDOWS

Football: QB Passing Yards
Football: WR Receiving Yards
Football: RB Rushing Yards
Football: Made Field Goals
Basketball: Total Player Points
Basketball: Total Player Rebounds
Basketball: Total Player Points + Rebounds
Basketball: Player Assists

For example you can take one receiver over 72 yards in one sportsbook at -115 and take him under 89 yards in another sportsbook at -110. Here you are hoping he gets in between 72 and 89 yards for the game. You can also find middling situations in regular spreads in basketball, for example, by wagering over 180.5 and under 183. I do not recommend doing these because they are very hard to win, unless you get a big window of at least 3 points with -110 juice.

Below I have listed many of the money odds you will get by calculating two different money lines in a special window. It is a good reference chart to use when these situations come up. You can see at a glance what the financial payout will be, and you can determine whether the window is worthwhile. I listed them roughly in order of the most common money lines available.

COMMON MONEY LINES

Money Line Figures Turned Into Real Time Odds	
-110 and −115 = 16 to 1	-110 and −150 = 6.67 to 1
-110 and −110 = 20 to 1	-120 and −130 = 8 to 1
-115 and −115 = 13.33 to 1	-120 and −135 = 7.27 to 1
-115 and −120 = 11.43 to 1	-125 and −135 = 6.67 to 1
-115 and −125 = 10 to 1	-130 and −135 = 6.15 to 1
-120 and −110 = 13.33 to 1	-140 and −145 = 4.71 to 1
-120 and −120 = 10 to 1	-150 and −140 = 4.44 to 1
-120 and −125 = 8.88 to 1	-120 and −165 = 4.71 to 1
-125 and −125 = 8 to 1	-150 and −170 = 3.33 to 1
-125 and −130 = 7.27 to 1	-160 and −185 = 2.76 to 1
-105 and −110 = 26.67 to 1	-140 and −155 = 4.21 to 1
-105 and −105 = 40 to 1	-160 and −160 = 3.33 to 1
-105 and −115 = 20 to 1	-130 and −130 = 6.67 to 1
-105 and −120 = 16 to 1	-175 and −185 = 2.5 to 1
-105 and −125 = 13.33 to 1	+115 and −125 = 20 to 1
-105 and −130 = 11.43 to 1	+110 and −130 = 20 to 1
-110 and −130 = 10 to 1	-150 and −160 = 3.64 to 1
-110 and −135 = 8.88 to 1	+125 and −150 = 16 to 1
-110 and −140 = 8 to 1	+130 and −170 = 10 to 1
-110 and −145 = 7.27 to 1	+110 and −110 = *****
*****There is no juice at all. You can balance it out to bet as much as you can, where you can win a lot of money, and risk nothing.	

Let's say you wager $500 at +110 = $550 and risk $550 at −110=$500. You are at least even if you go 1 and 1, and you are up $1,050 if you win both.

3. MAKE CONNECTED WAGERS

Connected wagers are similar to middling in that you are making multiple bets to pull in a potential profit. However, connected wagers are different from middling in that there is a legitimate chance of losing both (or more) wagers, although, of course, you think there is a better chance of winning both rather than losing both. Connected wagers always take place in the same sporting event, and are often prop bets.

Bets can be connected in many different ways. It's all about finding an angle on a game and finding connected wagers that fit with your angle. For example, you might think that an NFL game will be low scoring and decide to bet on that and each team's rushing touchdowns under 1 1/2. Or, going into game one of the 2005 NBA Finals, you could have bet Wallace, Hamilton and Prince under in points, knowing that they were playing a great defensive team. Your goal was that at least two out of three would go under so that you would make money. If all three bets won, you would make more money.

Any time that one wager is connected to another one, you are making a connected wager.

Here is an example of a connected wager that I bet years ago in the 1999 NBA Finals. The Knicks were playing San Antonio. However, Patrick Ewing was injured and would not play, and Larry Johnson would be playing with a hurt knee, making him suspect in his potential to score. There were lines for scoring points on the Knicks, Houston, and Sprewell. The line was set at 18 points on each of them.

With Ewing out and Johnson hurt, Houston and Sprewell would be counted on to do most of the scoring. Even though they were up against the league's best defense, I thought that I had a good set of wagers at hand. I bet them both over, thinking that at least one of them would have to score 20 points; maybe both of them. Not surprisingly, both players took a lot of shots. I easily won one of the bets, and I barely won the second.

Sometimes you find a football game with a high spread, perhaps one in which one team is favored by 20 points with the total for the game at only 41 points. A strategy can be to take the underdog +20 and the game over. The thinking is that the only way the favorite will cover 20 points is if the game goes over 40 points. In that case, you are hoping for a final score of 28-14 or something like 31-17 so that you win both bets.

You can make these kinds of bets, but make sure they are truly connected. Don't get too complex in overanalyzing a spread or game. Either it looks good or it does not. Be sure to balance the risk-versus-reward ratio, and bet within your range. Only make the connected wagers if you think you have an angle or edge and the set of wagers stand out.

4. BET A REALISTIC WINDOW OF ESTIMATED OUTCOMES

You can look at sports bets as very good wagers, others as good bets, while still other bets you may think are a total toss-up that can go either way. You can look at the statistics, the standings, a team's recent ATS, or other factors to decide. Another way at looking at some spreads is by looking at them with a realistic window. By *realistic window*, I mean the estimated range that you think the final score will fit into.

Let me give you an example. In the 2005 NBA season, the Los Angeles Clippers played the Memphis Grizzlies on February 3rd. Heading into the contest, both teams had key offensive players injured. Memphis had their best player out in Pau Gasol, as well as Bonzi Wells and backup point guard Earl Watson. The Clippers had their best scorer out in Corey Maggette, as well as role player Kerry Kittles. Vegas put a spread on the game at a very low 171. A spread of 171 is only set for two stagnant defensive teams that are terrible at scoring. Memphis did have a few recent, low-scoring games, but they also had some high-scoring ones with the depleted lineup. The Clippers had played little defense in 2005, while Memphis was about average in both offense and defense.

The main key in betting this game was that both teams had a lot of offensive depth, so even though key players were out, many offensive players on the bench were ready to step in. I felt that players such as Marko Jaric, Stromille Swift, and others could easily help the game go over.

The game could have had a final score of 77-74, but I thought that the game's final total would be somewhere between 165 and 200. This is actually a big window, but it is what I used in this situation. Sure, there was a chance I could lose this bet, but I felt there was a much greater chance that I would win it. I thought that a realistic total low was 165. If the final was less than 170, I would lose. If it fell between 172 and 200 (or higher), I would win. My realistic window was 36 points, as 36 numbers fell between 165 and 200.

I wagered on the over and the game was even higher scoring then I thought, surpassing my window. All the bench players stepped up and played great offense, and both teams played little defense. If you got a line between 85 and 90, this was a perfect game to bet the second half over, as well. In the first half, 99 points were scored, and in the second half, 110, for a total of 209 points, with LA winning. The line of 171 had been way off.

"Who in the world would bet the under?" I wondered. When you can ask yourself that question, then you know you have a great bet.

With an estimated window, you are predicting that the game will fall into a certain estimated path, but you feel that the greater path is in your betting favor. It works well in props. My sports book once gave me a line of 5 points on Bruce Bowen of the Spurs in the playoffs. It was only 5 points because, in his last two games, Bowen had averaged only 2 1/2 points per game. However, he was still getting 30-plus minutes of playing time. He could have had another 2- or 3-point game, but realistically, there was a better chance he would go over 5. I thought that a realistic window for him on that game was 3 to 12 points. So, if he got 3 or 4 points, I would lose; 5 and I would push; 6 to 12 and I win. I liked that scenario. He finished with 10 points.

While you can never pinpoint exactly what a player's stats will be, you can estimate the range and come up with some good bets. If you see a running back's yards at a spread of 58 1/2 and you think his window is 45 to 90, you likely have a good bet.

Window thinking is best with props and over/unders, but you can also use it in basketball spreads. However, I advise against window thinking with baseball and hockey. Baseball games can get blown wide open, and hockey games are based on only a few sequences in a game, and the goalie's ability to make saves. These factors can destroy your bets.

Below is a list of the types of bets where window thinking works to your advantage, starting with the strongest.

- Proposition bets on individual players' stats
- Basketball over/unders
- Football over/unders
- Basketball team versus team spreads

5. MAKE FUTURE BETS

Long-term bets are usually more secure wagers because they have more room for error. When betting on an individual game, it's do-or-die: If your star player happens to have an off night, you lose. In the long run, however, a star player will usually meet expectations.

Wagering on a team to win its division or the league championship is the most common future wager. My best advice is that if you want to bet on a team to win the championship, only bet on a legitimate, quality team. Do not get sucked in by great odds of 50 to 1, for example, on an average or worse-than-average team to win the title. It is not a good bet just because the odds are tempting.

Only bet on solid teams, no matter what the odds are. In the NBA, there are very few upsets; only about five teams have a legitimate shot at the title every year. These five teams can usually be determined by game 55 of the NBA season, if not sooner.

In the NFL, there has been a recent run of underdogs going all the way to the title because the league uses a one-game elimination format. In 2005, the Steelers, a 6-seed won the Super Bowl. In 2007, the NY Giants went on the road and went all the way to the title. In 2006, the Colts were 10 to 1 dogs before the playoffs to win the Super Bowl, but they came through and won it. In betting NFL futures heading into the playoffs, my advice is to never take a team at -120 to +250 to win it all. For you to make money, you are asking a team to win three or four do-or-die games against quality opponents at poor odds. I can find a -120 to +250 in one game. Either take a solid team with at least +400 or more, or don't make an NFL future wager.

In baseball, underdogs can go all the way to the title, like the Florida Marlins did in 2003 and the Los Angeles Angels in 2002, but you should still bet on solid teams that figure to at least make the playoffs. What is good about betting baseball championship futures is that there are no dominant favorites, so you can get a very good team at generous odds. In baseball, once you are in the playoffs you have a shot.

In hockey, probably more than in the other three major sports, betting underdogs to win the title can be a good bet. In 2003 Anaheim made it to the finals, and in 2004 Calgary did. Both were low 7-seeds. Even though they did not win it all, you could have made money in the finals just by hedging and betting on the other team. I know that the Anaheim and Calgary odds were as high as 40 to 1 and 70 to 1 against winning the cup at some point in their respective seasons.

CHAPTER 1

3 SPORTS BETTING CONCEPTS YOU MUST KNOW

1. THEY ARE NOT "DUE" FOR A WIN

There is no such thing as being "due" for a win in sports. No team gets a victory just for showing up. Eventually, hot streaks will burn out and cold streaks will thaw, but no one can predict when a streak will end. The reality is this: The better a team is playing, the better chance it has of winning its next game; the worse a team is playing, the better chance it has of losing its next game.

There are many reasons that could contribute to a losing streak. For example, maybe the players have banded together against their coach; maybe the team captain is playing hurt; maybe one player has ruined the team chemistry; or maybe a bunch of players have packed it in mentally and are already thinking about the off-season. A team that has lost six games in a row is not a good pick for the next game. They may snap out of it and win that next game, but the trend is that they are losing now, so don't look to bet against that trend. Even great teams hit cold streaks, and when they do, you should not be placing wagers on them. Wait until they are out of their cold slump. Just remember that a team is never "due."

2. GARBAGE TIME

Garbage time occurs when one team has an irreversible lead over the other and the coaches bring in bench players, some of whom rarely play in close games. In garbage time, effort and execution definitely are not at their best.

The two main sports in which garbage time is clearly linked to your sports wagers are football and basketball. Garbage time is a factor you have to consider when making your spread and prop bets. For example, suppose you really like one football team to blowout the other team, and your pick is a 10 1/2 point favorite. Your team has dominated the game and is up by 17 points going into the fourth quarter. But then your team gets conservative on offense and just punts the ball away in each possession. They still hold on to the 17-point lead until the final two minutes in garbage time, when their opponent comes back to score a meaningless touchdown. The result? The game winds up with a 10-point difference. This happens frequently in the NFL, which is why I don't often like to bet on NFL teams at minus big points. It seems as though your team has to get a 20-point lead in order for your -10.5 point spread bet to be secure!

Similar situations happen in basketball. You could take a team at -13 1/3 points in the NBA, but they could put the game on cruise control after being up by 16 points with three minutes left in the game. Then, both coaches clear their benches and bring in the second-tier players. Garbage time kicks in! Your team has dominated the whole way, but during garbage time if the team that is down 16 points outscores your team's scrubs by 4 points in those three minutes, your great-looking bet has gone bad. This happens all the time in the NBA. Also, remember that the team with the double-digit lead will generally not shoot if they get possession with less than 24 seconds on the game clock. They will just run out the remaining seconds on the clock, and pass the ball to the referee.

In the NBA, the quality of the bench during garbage time is important. Some NBA teams have a strong second unit, while other teams have no depth and a terrible bench. In the 2002-2003 season, the Sacramento Kings had a great bench that featured Bobby Jackson, Hedo Turkoglu, Keon Clark, Scot Pollard and Gerald Wallace. That's a pretty good five players to have playing garbage time for you, and it's one of the reasons why the Kings blew a lot of teams out that season. If you envision a game going to garbage time and you're thinking of taking that team at -11.5 points, be sure to factor in the quality of their bench and how they usually play when they're up 16 with three minutes left.

The garbage-time factor is even more important when betting props than it is with regular bets. Garbage time can seriously affect the result of your props because it can limit the playing time of your star players. A player averaging 40 minutes a game may only get 30 minutes in a game if his team is blowing out its opponent. Jerry Sloan, the Utah Jazz coach, used to rest John Stockton if the team was up by big points. You cannot predict when a game will be so lopsided, but a good indicator is the spread. Any game where a team is favored by 10 points or more, especially at home, could indicate a greater than average chance of garbage time.

For example, let's say that Kobe Bryant and the Lakers are playing the Charlotte Bobcats, a last-place team, at home. The Lakers are favored by 10 points, and Kobe is averaging 28 points and 42 minutes a game on the season. You may see a prop on him at 27 1/2 points. An average gambler may think, "Wow, Kobe is playing such a weak team that he's going to kill them for at least 30 points." Wrong. Kobe may easily play a team game with his team up by 20 points, but in garbage time he will be on the bench, having played only 33 of 48 minutes and finishing with 21 points and 8 assists.

Great players usually take over when they have to, not when they have a big lead. Betting under may be a good bet in this situation. Superstar players will usually get a lot more points during close games, because that's when the rest of the team gets the ball to them and expects them to step up and score. If they get enough shots, they usually will score. But during blowouts, they just pass the ball around and try to get other players involved in the offense. As I mentioned earlier, many of Michael Jordan's 50-point games were in close contests.

When I bet a prop, I look at the game and the spread individually. I envision how I think that game will go, and after, I analyze the prop, remembering that garbage time can take a great bet and turn it into a losing one. It can also take a bet that didn't look so good and make it a winner due to last-second garbage points. College basketball sometimes has a lot of garbage time, as games with 15 to 20 point spreads come up often, so watch out. Garbage time is something else to think about when you're looking for good or great wagers in games that involve big spreads.

3. BE VERY CONCERNED IF YOU ARE GETTING KILLED ON BIG BETS

In sports gambling, you have to believe that every bet you make gives you some kind of advantage. Either you are finding and making quality wagers, or you are not. If you are consistently making good bets you should not be going on significant losing streaks. You should be winning your share of bets.

All gamblers go through ups and downs in their gaming careers. When you lose bets that were very close to being winners, you should always consider whether you made a bad wager. But don't get upset if you lose a really close bet, by 1 point for example. Here's why.

In the 2004 NFL Playoffs, the New England Patriots were playing the Tennessee Titans at home in a do–or–die game. The over/under in the game was low; the line started at about 36, but dropped down to 33.5 before kickoff. I did the research and analysis on the game and I really liked the over.

Here is why I liked the over:

When the two teams played each other earlier in the regular season, they combined for 68 points in a high scoring shoot-out.

In large part, the spread was based on the weather forecast for the game. Snow or freezing rain had been predicted, which would have helped make the game be low scoring. When I checked the forecast 30 minutes before the game, it had changed: There was going to be no snow or rain, although it was going to be cold in New England.

Two of the best quarterbacks in the NFL were playing, Steve McNair and Tom Brady. Further, both teams preferred passing over running, and passing always leads to more scoring.

The game was going well for me early—the weather was pretty good, and while the field was a bit rugged because of the cold weather, it was not enough to seriously affect the play of the game. Only the kicking game had been disrupted a little bit. By halftime New England was winning 14 to 7, so all I needed was 13 points in the second half and I would win. My bet was looking pretty good.

I actually could have hedged my bet at halftime and bet the second half under 18, thus ensuring that I at least would win one bet and lose one, and still have a chance to win both if the final total in the game ended up between 34 and 41 points. I decided not to hedge, because I thought that they could easily go over the 18.

In the third quarter, Tennessee got 7 points and tied the game at 14. Now all I needed was 6 points in the fourth quarter to win my bet, two field goals or one touchdown. But two or three plays did not go my way, and I lost a very close bet. The final score was 17 to 14 in New England's favor. 3 more points and I would have won! Tennessee was driving for the tying field goal late when, on fourth down, Drew Bennett, a Titan wide receiver, buttered a sure first-down catch with great field position. I only lost my bet by a play or two, which was better than having lost the bet with a score of 13-7, for example.

To me, losing a close bet is much better then getting killed. Why? If you are losing your bets by large margins, that is a sign that you are not making good wagers. You must look at the factors on which you are basing your bets, and examine your analysis.

3 Sports Betting Concepts You Must Know

My New England/Tennessee over bet was in a position to win, so I had a good chance of cashing in.

If your bets consistently don't even get in position to win, you are doing something wrong. If you bet big on an NFL road team at -4 points and they lose the game by 30 points, you can conclude that your bet might not have been good. This will happen to everyone from time to time, but when you look back at losses you've suffered when you bet a substantial amount of money, most of them should be close losses. A close loss is a sign that it just wasn't your day. If you stay consistent and do your homework, you will win your share of close bets in the long run.

Financially, a loss is a loss, but you shouldn't look at it that way. Your success in the long term will be based on making well thought-out picks. When selecting wagers, putting yourself in a good position to win is half the battle. Sometimes it just won't be your turn to win because of a game-changing play here or there. Those days will balance out in the long run. Do not get discouraged by last-second dramatics: I have seen some crazy plays go in my favor, while others have gone against me. Stay positive and you will be okay.

If your bets are getting killed, you must reanalyze your research, reexamine your theories, and lower both the cash amount of your bets and the number of total bets you are making. Do this until you learn from your mistakes, because if you don't, you will lose too much money. The key is to be able to differentiate between a good bet and a great bet, and to be able to put more of your money on your great wagers. This is the most important thing I can tell you!

Regardless of the quality of the bet or how much you bet on it, all of your final scores and betting results can be graded after the game is over, and will fall into one these six categories:

BETTING RESULTS GRADES

WIN

A) You kill your wager, blow the spread out, and win easily, coasting away with the bet.

B) Your bet was in decent control the whole way, covering most of the game, and your bet finished the game with a solid win.

C) You win a close bet. With a play or plays here or there, the final result may have, or easily could have, gone the other way.

LOSE

D) You lose a close bet. With a play or plays here or there, the final result may have, or easily could have, gone the other way.

F) Your bet was never in control. You were behind most of the way, and your bet finished up as a solid loser with few chances of a late comeback.

F-) Your bet got killed and you were blown away. You lost easily and were never in it.

After each wager, grade it and record the grade in the chart you keep of all your bets. It is wise to recap each of your wagers to see how you did so you can truly see if you are making sound decisions as a sports handicapper. This is also a way to learn what your strengths are and to learn from your mistakes so that the next time a similar bet comes your way, you may know to bet bigger, bet smaller, bet the same amount, or not bet at all. If most of the wagers that you win barely cover the spread or barely win, you will not make money in the long term. A good wager will beat the spread solidly and a great wager will destroy the spread.

Your biggest and greatest wagers should end up with mostly A or B results, with some C and D results. Your good bets should end up with mostly B grades, some A grades, a solid combination of C and D grades, with a few F grades sprinkled in. Consistent grades of F are for people who lose money sports gambling. Yes, everyone will have an occasional F result, but you should have few F's in your biggest wagers. If you find that a lot of your big bets are getting killed, you must regroup and stop betting big until you can differentiate between a bad, a good and a great wager.

CHAPTER 12

7 STRATEGIES FOR WAGERING ON TEAM SPORTS

1. BET ON TEAMS YOU CAN TRUST

One of the basics of winning money at sports betting is to wager on players and, more importantly, teams that you believe are great and can rely on for a consistent performance. The bottom line is to look for teams and players that are consistent and that you believe are winners. Almost any pro team can stay close in a game, but what sets apart the great teams and great players from the average ones is that the great ones make plays when they count, when the game is on the line. These plays are often the ones that make or break your close wager.

Many sporting events are anybody's game with three minutes left, but the good teams usually find a way to win, and the bad teams find a way to lose in close games. The good teams and players execute while the poor teams and poor players do not execute down the stretch. Any pro team can keep a game close against another pro team, but can you rely on them to come through down the stretch? That is often the question that will decide your bet.

I once bet on the Buffalo Bills to beat the Miami Dolphins on Monday Night Football. The Bills were 6-point underdogs, but early in the season, they were showing that they were just as good a team as Miami, if not better. I placed the wager because I really believed in Doug Flutie, the quarterback of the Bills. In my mind, Flutie was a winner—he had been a winner in college winning the Rose Bowl with Boston College, and a winner in the Canadian Football League winning Grey Cups. Whenever I saw him play, he made few mistakes. I thought that Buffalo could win because they were equally as talented as Miami, and my quarterback, Flutie, was a player who would perform well. Even if Buffalo lost by 3 to 5 points in a close game, I would still win with the points. Buffalo went on to win the game outright, covering the spread and, as I predicted, Flutie played extremely well, making no mistakes.

Sometimes, sports gambling comes down to betting on the money players. Bet on the players and teams that have shown you solid play and consistency during the season, leading you to trust them for future performance.

On the other hand, quarterback Kurt Warner—yes, Kurt Warner—has had some great seasons in the NFL, but because of his knack for throwing interceptions, I find it hard to bet on his teams, especially when they are big favorites. Warner either plays very well or he can play a stinker game with four or five interceptions. This inconsistency does not happen with Tom Brady and Peyton Manning.

The NBA is a superstar league: Rarely will a team have any success without having at least one great player on its roster. The teams that win the close games are the ones that have a great player, a player who will make a great shot or create a great shot for his teammates in the last few minutes of a game. In a close game in the NBA, the team that has the best player on the court has the advantage at the end of the game. That is how Lebron James carried his team to the NBA finals in the 2006-2007 season. His team kept most playoff games close and in the last few minutes, he would just take over the game. If two NBA teams are evenly matched, I will almost always favor the team that has the big superstar. Always be careful when betting against legends such as Lebron James or Kobe Bryant in games that have a small point spread. These guys have such a will to win that, in a close game, they will find a way to win.

During the 2002-2003 NBA season, I once bet on the Denver Nuggets, one of the worst teams in basketball, as an 11-point underdog against a mediocre team. I needed them to lose by 11 or less. They played poorly on offense and just came short of what I needed. It was not a terrible bet, but after, a friend of mine made a good point. He said, "Do you know why you lost? You lost because you bet on the Nuggets." That made a lot of sense. I put my money in the wrong hands. It was as simple as that. Regardless of the spread, you want to put your money in good hands.

You don't want to be the person who bets against a great team in a big game, either. Unless you have a strong reason in betting against them, why bet against a great team? A better option is to be patient and find games where you bet against garbage teams. For example, in 2005, a lot of the public bet on Indianapolis to beat New England in the playoffs. The line moved from starting at about New England -2 to a closing line of Indy at -1. New England dominated Indianapolis in a defensive battle in cold, snowy weather, by a score of 20-3. Why be that person to bet against the champs at home and lay a point or two when there are better bets out there to make? It's usually best to avoid games involving two great teams where the spread is 3 points or less, so I didn't touch that game.

Here's a basic, yet important tip: In all sports, the team that wins the game covers the spread more often than not. All point-spread underdogs that win the game obviously cover the spread; and common sense will tell you that favorites that win the game are more likely to cover than not cover.

Before you make any wager, you have to ask yourself, "Am I confident putting money on the game?" Will you be happy with your decision, win or lose? If the answer is yes, go ahead with the wager; if the answer is no, look elsewhere.

2. BET ON PLAYERS YOU CAN TRUST

The most important positions in the four major sports are quarterback (football), goaltender (hockey) and starting pitcher (baseball). In basketball, there is often one star player that would be equivalent to the roles mentioned above. Always factor in these players when making any bet.

3. TRENDS VERSUS SYSTEMS

A *system* of betting usually involves making wagers based on stats from prior games. With a system, a sports handicapper is very set in his betting pattern. Wagering with a *trend* is when you see some change in the sports wagering market and you look to take advantage of the change by making wagers with the trend. You might detect a trend when you see a very hot team, or a very cold team, or some over/under spreads that are not accurate for a certain team. A trend can also be found after a major trade takes place, thus changing the dynamic of two teams. With trends you make a set of wagers with the trend, hoping to capitalize.

I am a big believer in wagering with trends but I am not a believer in making wagers based on a system. Yes, some systems work, but finding a system that wins consistently is very tough.

Trends can be found in each league. The key is for you to be able to pick up on a trend and find the discrepancy in the spreads being produced. Here is an example of a system versus a trend. A system would be wagering with the spread against all NBA teams that are playing four games in five nights against a team that's over .500 and wagering an exact amount of money against them in the fourth game. A trend would be wagering on the Chicago Bulls' games under, due to a recent trade that gave them a lot of defensive players, causing them to have problems scoring. With this trend, I wagered different amounts based on how much I liked each game; but once the spreads got too low, I stop making this set of wagers.

Here is the main difference between the system and the trend. In the system, you are not specific enough in what you like. You are basing your bets on the notion that teams that have played four games in five nights will be tired, and will be hard pressed to beat a good team. The problem is that Vegas incorporated those factors into the spread. There is no real advantage; the system is too random. In the system, you are wagering against that team regardless of the spread. My trend wager above was good because I found an inequity in the spread based on the team's personnel change. From game to game, I decided how much to wager. Once the high spreads were reduced, my trend ended and I looked to make wagers elsewhere.

The key is to be able to find a trend that right away gives you an inequality with the spread. When the spreads got too high, you stop betting on them.

Now, let's look at a perfect example of wagering with trends in the NFL. In the 2007 NFL season, the New England Patriots went 16-0 in the regular season, a remarkable, undefeated, regular season campaign. Interestingly, there was ample opportunity to bet on the Patriots and against the Patriots that season. Amazingly, the Patriots won their first eight games by an average margin of 25 points per game, and they were able to cover the spread in all eight of these games. They destroyed opponents with their historic passing attack featuring Tom Brady and Randy Moss. Vegas could not make the spreads in Patriots games big enough, and they kept blowing teams out. If you had picked up on this trend after a few weeks, you would have found some games during their run in which you could have made good money.

However, the Patriots' final eight games of the regular season were a different story; they were only able to cover the point spread in two of those eight games. What caused the sudden change? First of all, the results of New England's first eight games caused the spreads in their last eight contests to become overinflated. They had games in which they were favored by 20 points or more, way too high for any team to consistently cover. Secondly, the weather became a factor. The Patriots had put up big points with their passing game. In the first eight games of the season, during September and October, they played in mostly clear conditions. In their last eight games, during November and December, the Pats played some games in very cold, windy, mucky conditions. It is hard to cover big point spreads in winter with windy conditions, especially when you rely on the passing game so much. Thirdly, the NFL is a league with a lot of parity.

It was only a matter of time before opponents learned how to adjust to the Patriots game.

I was able to target three games in which I thought that spread was too high, and made money on them. In Week 10 against Baltimore, in Baltimore, New England was a 21-point favorite. I knew that Baltimore was a great bet. New England had squeaked by Philly the week before, looking human; and the weather forecast called for heavy winds, so I knew that it would be tough on New England's passing attack. Also, Baltimore had a reputation for having a stingy defense. It is unbelievably difficult to cover 21 points on the road during winter playing conditions against a tough defense—very difficult. Baltimore almost won the game straight up, but fell 27-24.

In Week 15, the New York Jets were 20 1/2 point dogs on the road in New England. Once again, the weather forecast called for a cold winter day. The Jets played tough and lost 20-10. The third game I liked was Indianapolis +5 at home against New England in Week 9. My thinking was that both teams were undefeated at the time. I could easily see Indy winning the game, but I also could see them losing by 1 to 4 points in a close contest. Indy controlled most of the game, but New England stole it at the end, 24-20, and I was able to cover my spread.

These were three great wagers because the spreads on each game were inflated and the weather made it tough to cover in two of the games. (Ironically, New England did not cover the spread in their three playoff games, either.) I didn't love these wagers only because of the spread; I really thought that my teams would be able to compete and put up a fight against the Patriots in all three games. In Week 16, I actually passed on betting the Dolphins at +20 points because I thought they could easily get smashed by over 30 points.

The Patriots were a perfect example of trend betting in 2007. There was money to be made by wagering on them and against them by identifying the trend and choosing the right games within those two eight-game intervals. On the other hand, a systems bettor may have decided after Week 6 to wager on the Patriots each week with the spread, regardless of the its point differential, for the rest of the season. And he would have ended up losing money.

Look for trends, taking into account injuries, a red-hot team, an ice-cold team, trades, or even a new coach. If you believe that a team has become overhyped or underrated, you may have found a good trend and the spreads in that team's games may be off. Look for changes in style and performance, and translate them into a trend that turns into a profit. Other possibilities of trends occur when a star player in the NBA gets hurt and his team starts losing every game, or maybe a key quarterback gets injured and his team starts losing games by big points. Often, these injuries and changes are not adequately reflected in the spread.

Your job is to find the trend and make money.

4. NEW COACH EQUALS TEAM CHANGE

A coaching change during a sports season can be significant. The new coach could have a totally different approach from the old coach, and you could capitalize on that with good bets. For example, a very good defensive NBA team could fire the coach and then hire an offensive coach to take over. Suddenly, the team may be putting up bigger numbers with the new coach because they're running and gunning. For the first few games, you may be able to get the spreads that were based on the team's previous style of play. Look for some type of edge if the new basketball or football coach announces some kind of new style.

A good example occurred when Chicago fired coach Bill Cartwright and hired Scott Skiles. With the aid of a trade, Chicago acquired Antonio Davis and Jerome Williams. Suddenly, they changed dramatically from an offensive team to a team that focused on defense. They became a very low scoring team, a defensive team. In the subsequent few weeks, Bulls' games consistently went under the over/under total.

In all four major sports—hockey, baseball, football or basketball—hiring a new coach seems to have a honeymoon effect during which the team suddenly goes on a decent winning streak. This is due to four factors.

The players may have lost respect for the old coach, but the new coach is able to motivate his new team.

The players know that if they don't step up their game, they may lose playing time, or may even lose their jobs. When a new coach comes on board, the regulars tend to start playing harder, and bench players see the change as an opportunity to play more, so they step up their game if they are given a chance to play.

Players really respond to a change in game plan or strategy that the new coach puts in place.

Overall, morale tends to be higher whenever a new coach takes over a team.

A perfect example of this occurred during the 2003-2004 NBA season when the New Jersey Nets fired Coach Byron Scott, who was feuding with some of the key players on the team. Assistant Lawrence Frank was chosen to take over the team. Frank did not change any of the major strategies in the way that the team played, but he did bring a sense of fun and relaxation back to the team. The Nets went on a 13-game winning streak to start off Frank's coaching career! The players obviously loved the new atmosphere.

When a new coach is hired, if you see that a certain player's minutes have increased or decreased substantially, look for point props that you can bet under or over.

A new coach can be a factor, as it was in 2004-2005 when George Karl took over for Denver at the all-star break. The team responded by winning 80 percent of its remaining regular season games, going 32-8 with Karl—a big increase from their prior sub-45 percent winning record.

5. BIG TEAMS CAN BE UNJUSTLY FAVORED

Remember that the line set up by Vegas is designed to stimulate equal wagering on both sides; it is not always designed based on the strengths of the two teams. Often, big name or popular teams will become big favorites just because of their popularity. Over the years, many sports teams have been given too much credit in the point spread. For example, in college football, Notre Dame has often received too much credit because of its big name, and has often been favored against teams with a lot more talent.

Going back to the late 90s, Duke played Connecticut in the NCAA championship game. Duke was a very popular team at the time, with three or four future NBA players on the roster. However, Connecticut was a great team as well, and also had some future pros. They had beaten Duke earlier in the season. The game was played on a neutral court and Duke was favored by 9 1/2 points, way too big of a spread. I bet on Connecticut, who not only covered the spread, but won the game outright by 3 points.

Another example of a high spread occurred in the 2005 Super Bowl with New England versus Philadelphia. The line opened at 6.5, then quickly moved to 7 and stayed there until kickoff. Philly was a great team, just as good as New England, in my opinion. Philly had really only lost one full-squad game all year; in the last two games, the team was resting starters because they had already clinched the home-field advantage. New England would be favored by 7 points to a great Philly team that was 15-1 on the year (including playoffs to that point) in games that mattered.

New England was a great team at the time, but not a dominating team. The Pats were a team that won close games due to great coaching by Bill Belichick and terrific teamwork. When I saw Terrell Owens, an impact player, look pretty good in practice a few days before the game—he had been doubtful earlier—I knew it was a solid bet. Vegas and the public did not realize how big a factor he would be. The line did not move after it was confirmed that Owens would play. I bet big money on Philly at +7 1/2 points, buying the extra half a point. I actually got +7 1/2 and -110 by shopping around for a good line.

I thought that one of four things would happen:

1. Philly would win by more than 7 points
2. Philly would win by 1 to 7 points
3. New England would win by 1 to 7 points
4. New England would win by more than 7 points

I thought that I had a great chance of winning my bet. I also thought that option two or three had a great chance of happening as well. I could win the bet through the front door if Philly won the game or just kept it close. I also could win through the backdoor if Philly was down by 8 to 14 points late and scored late to cover the spread.

What happened? Philly was in the game the whole way, up by 7 points early, tied at the half at 7-7, and finally losing by 3 points, 24 to 21. The Eagles scored a late, backdoor touchdown as the Patriots played conservatively, ahead by 10, and Philly covered the spread. I won my bet through the backdoor, even though it was not easy. Terrell Owens had an amazing game, racking up a lot of yardage and moving the chains on a lot of Eagles drives. Without Owens in that game, I don't think Philadelphia would have covered the spread, but with him in it, Philadelphia was able to compete.

I couldn't understand why people loved taking New England at -7. That is a bet I would never have made because Philadelphia was just as talented. In fact, if the spread in the game had been New England -3, I still would have not bet on New England.

Another lopsided opportunity presented itself in the 1998 Super Bowl when the Green Bay Packers were favored by 12 points against the Denver Broncos. That line was way off. It actually opened at 14 and then slowly moved a few points before kickoff. That big line was in place because the NFC had won the previous 15 or so Super Bowls and Green Bay was the defending champion. People thought that the NFC would dominate again. But how could Green Bay have been favored by 14 points on a neutral field? This is a perfect illustration of why you should not look at history. Denver had not played Green Bay in the previous 15 Super Bowls, so any spread based on that history was invalid. Denver was equally as talented as Green Bay. No matter what had happened in the past, smart handicappers realized that it was not the NFC playing the AFC; it was Green Bay versus Denver. Denver went on to win the game outright by 7 points.

As always, you are looking for good value. When you believe that a team is unjustifiably favored based on their big name or past results, or because Vegas is trying to balance the books, you have an opportunity.

6. BET AGAINST TEAMS RESTING KEY PLAYERS

In the four major sports, there comes a time at the end of each season when some teams have already clinched their position in the playoffs. When this happens, the team often rests players, or doesn't give 100 percent. You can take advantage by betting on the team that needs the win, as opposed to the better team since the other team does not really care whether they win or lose. You have to pick the right situation, of course. For example, suppose you find that one team in the NBA needs a win to make the playoffs, and their record on the year is 40 and 41 going in to their final game of the season. You also see that the team they are facing is already out of the playoffs with a record of 36 and 45. There's a good chance that the 36-win team will still be trying to win the game. Acting as a spoiler, their attitude may be, "If we're not going to the playoffs, then you're not going to make the playoffs, either." They will play loose and try to take some solace in knocking the other team out of the playoffs.

Look for a team that is fighting to make the playoffs, or fighting its way up the standings, or a team that is strongly playing out the stretch versus a team that has already clinched and cannot move up or down the standings, no matter what, for the rest of the season. The team that has clinched its position will often not be playing at 100 percent of their potential and might also be resting key players.

How do you utilize the strategy? Read as many previews of the game as possible or research the team you are betting against. Often, the coaches and managers will tip their hands and tell you whether they will be resting key players the day before the game. You can also look at these coaches' histories in games that did not matter. Read box scores and recaps of previous seasons games to see what they did the last time they were coaching a game that had no effect on their playoff positioning

In these scenarios, the key is knowing in advance that the team that has already clinched its playoff position will be resting key players. I once wagered on the Milwaukee Bucks in the second-to-last game of the regular season. They were at home against the Pistons, who were resting two of their best players in preparation for the playoffs. The Bucks, only 6-point favorites, went on to destroy the Pistons by 20 points and the Pistons didn't even care. I can recall many games where one team was resting its starters and I profitably bet at the end of the NBA season.

A key part of this strategy is analyzing the strength of a team's bench. If you know that the team's bench has little talent, chances are good that they will get creamed. But if they have a good bench, they may be able to compete even if the game has no meaning to them.

At the end of the 2007-2008 NBA season, I lost a few bets by wagering against the Boston Celtics. The Celtics had already clinched the best record in the NBA with a handful of games left to the season. In some games, they rested their three best players, Garnett, Allen and Pierce. I underestimated how strong the Celtics bench players were. Boston won two road games in Atlanta and New York that had no meaning to them. The Celtics bench players stepped up and played amazing ball down the stretch. Looking back, I still feel that they were good wagers, but of course, you can't win every bet, even though the bets might be strong. While the Celtics cost me a few wagers at the end of the season, I was not worried because, overall, I do very well at the end of each NBA season. I learned to be leery of very strong bench play at the end of the year with resting teams.

A perfect example of a team resting its starters in the NFL was the Philadelphia Eagles of 2004. The Eagles were a dominant football team. Through 14 weeks, they compiled a record of 13-1 and had clinched home field advantage all the way to the Super Bowl. They played their last two games of the season against two average teams (at best), St. Louis and Cincinnati. In the first game they were 4 1/2-point underdogs at St. Louis. The coach rested his starting quarterback, Donovan McNabb, after the first series and they went on to get killed 20-7, not putting up any kind of a fight. Even with this lackluster effort, they were only 3-point underdogs at home against Cincinnati the next week. Again, with nothing to play for, Philly rested its starting quarterback, running back and key defensive players and went on to get killed 38 to 10. I capitalized by betting against them with a good spread as Philly's backup quarterback played terribly. In these situations, the game often comes down to the quarterback. If a team has a quality backup quarterback, it may not be such a good bet; but if they have a weak backup, chances are they will lose handily.

When you find all their key players on a team playing big minutes, versus a team that does not need the win, but is more concerned about getting through the game without an injury and staying fresh, then you are in an excellent position to make money! Remember that you are dealing with pro athletes who all have talent; if one team doesn't care to win, the other team can often dominate them. This end-of-the-season strategy works best in basketball and second best in football where quarterbacks may be rested. It also works somewhat in baseball where key players won't even see the plate.

One final, extreme example: A situation came up where a team would be better positioned if it lost the last game of the regular season. In the 1997 NBA season, the Phoenix Suns were battling for the sixth and seventh playoff spot in the Western Conference. The Suns were a very small athletic team with Jason Kidd, Kevin Johnson and Steve Nash; their coach often played three or four guards at once. If they finished sixth they would play the third seed; if they finished seventh, the two seed. At the time, the third seed was the Houston Rockets, a very big and experienced team with Barkley, Drexler and Olajuwon. The second seed was Seattle, a very similar team to Phoenix, small and athletic. Phoenix thought that they matched up better against Seattle and didn't want to go up against a big Houston team. Their last game of the year at home was against one of the worst teams in the league, the Vancouver Grizzlies. Phoenix got killed by over 20 points. Why? They played their bench players for big minutes right away and their starters barely played. The strategy actually worked out well: They took Seattle to a deciding fifth game, and they almost won the series.

In the NBA, start looking for these opportunities from mid- to late- April, and in the NFL start looking in December; but remember not to bet against a spoiler that is playing with nothing to lose. When you find a team that has already clinched a playoff position and will be resting players, not giving 100 percent mentally, you have a good opportunity to make a profit by betting against that team.

BET WITH
- Team trying to clinch playoff spot or gain seeding in stand-ings by winning
- Spoiler: Team that is out of playoffs playing loose and strong down the stretch

BET AGAINST
- Team that is resting key players for playoffs and is locked in to their position in the standings

---

7. BET ON A PLAYOFF SERIES

Wagering on a playoff series often can be a great financial op-portunity. When betting a series, the advantage is that one play or one game will not beat you. There is more security in that a team has to beat you three out of five or four out of seven times for you to lose your bet. However, if you like betting on underdogs, you are sometimes better off taking the individual game, because it is likelier that an underdog will win one game than four.

You should feel more secure taking a team to win a *series* at -400 than taking a team in one *game* at -400. Single-game upsets happen quite often, but in a best-of-seven series, the better team will generally win. Now that the NBA has gone to the best-of-seven first-round series instead of the best of five, it has put the underdog at a bigger disadvantage because they have to win four games instead of three.

That one extra game makes a big difference. In the 2003 NBA playoffs, I bet on Detroit to beat Orlando in the first round of the playoffs. Detroit was the number-1 seed, Orlando the number-8 seed. I did not bet it based on how they were seeded; I bet on Detroit because I thought that they were a much better team that played tough defense and efficient offense. I also thought that Orlando was a soft, finesse, one-man team that wasn't built for the playoffs. Detroit was -210 to win the series, odds that I thought were good. I gave Orlando little chance to win the series.

Orlando won Game 1 in Detroit. If I had bet big on Detroit, the favorite, for the one game, I would have lost. But I had bet that Orlando would not win *four* games. Orlando lost Game 2 in Detroit, then went back to Orlando and won both games there to take a 3 to 1 lead. If it had been a best-of-five series, I would have lost. Actually, if it had been a five game series, I would not have bet as big. The underdog has such an advantage in a best of five: All they need is to get a split on the road in the first two games, because an underdog can win two straight games at home. The best of five puts a lot of pressure on the home team.

Detroit blew out Orlando by over 30 points in Game 5, then played strong and won Game 6 by double digits. Going into Game 7, I was very confident. Detroit blew Orlando out, at 1 point having a lead of over 25 points. At the end I was right with Detroit, but it had been a lot closer than I thought it would be.

When betting on a series, look to hedge your wager in the right situation. If your team has a 3 to 2 lead in the series and you are worried that they can still lose it, you can wager on the other team to win the series. By hedging you will put yourself into a position to profit either way. Lots of teams have come back over the years from a 3 to 2 deficit.

Let's say that the Utah Jazz are playing the New Orleans Hornets in the NBA playoffs and you really like New Orleans to win the series. New Orleans is +120 to win the series and you decide to wager $500 on New Orleans to win $600. They play well and have a 3 to 2 series lead going into Game 6 at home. Utah is +280 to win the series. You can now wager $178.57 at +280 ($500) on Utah to win. If Utah wins the series, you are even: You have won $500 back on Utah and have at least covered your original bet. If New Orleans wins the series, you will still be up an overall profit of $421.43. Either way, if New Orleans wins Game 6 or 7, you are up $421.43. If they end up losing the series, you saved your $500 bet and ended up even, not a bad position to be in.

You can hedge to cancel out your bet, to minimize risk, or to guarantee a profit. It is up to you, based on how you see the series going. Overall, hedging is great when the odds are in your favor and there is still reasonable risk. Either way, you can use hedging to your advantage.

CHAPTER 13

8 TOP TIPS FOR BETTING FOOTBALL

1. AN EFFECTIVE NFL BETTING STRATEGY

Bettors have many different theories on how to bet NFL football. You may like to wager on certain NFL games because you like a team, or because you really believe that the game will go over or under. Some people say things such as, "Take the Jets in Week 1. They're 14-6 against the spread over the last 20 years on opening night." Or, "Take Green Bay at home; they cover the spread in 62 percent of their home games." Or maybe, "Take New England at -9.5 points. The Pats are a dominant team and they're playing Miami, who is 9-23 the last two years against the spread!"

How a team has fared in the past 20 years or past two years against the spread on opening night should have no bearing on how you bet the upcoming game. What do you care if the New York Jets are 70 percent against the spread the last two years?

That has no bearing on whether they will cover the spread this Sunday. Why would you care if, hypothetically, the Oakland Raiders are 24-9 lifetime on Monday Night Football? They may have earned that record because they played great football in the past, but that does not mean that they are a great team now.

All your thoughts should be focused on how both teams have played in recent games.

The way I see the NFL today, there are four different caliber levels of teams:

GROUP 1) DOMINANT TEAMS
These teams have great quarterback play, solid talent, great coaching, and solid defenses. They destroy poor teams and usually end up winning between 12 and 15 games.

GROUP 2) GOOD SOLID TEAMS
These teams have good quarterback play but not usually great, are competitive every week, and find a way to win close games because of their solid overall play. They usually finish the season at 9 to 11 wins.

GROUP 3) AVERAGE TEAMS
These teams are average, no matter how you look at them. Some weeks, they have good quarterback play; some weeks, poor. They can beat the bad teams consistently, but cannot beat good or dominant teams on a regular basis. They usually finish the season with 6 to 8 wins.

GROUP 4) WEAK TEAMS
These teams have the worst quarterbacks in the league. They can only beat weak teams like themselves with the exception of

the once-a-year upset. They usually will finish the season with 1 to 5 wins.

Of course, some teams overachieve and others underachieve during the season. A team's record at a given point may not be an indication of how good they really are, or how bad they really are. Check to see whether these teams are keeping games close or are getting blown out, and try to determine which category a team really falls into.

My strategy is simple: I usually bet only Groups 2 and 3. Whenever you can find two teams that are playing each other that fall into the same group (either both in group two or both in group three) and you can get a spread of between +6 to +9 points or more, take the underdog. Ideally you are looking for +7 to +9. Seven is the key number in football. The idea is to bet on a game between good or average teams of similar caliber, but ones that are not dominant so that you will always have a chance to cover the spread.

Groups 1 and 4 are not what I look for in this strategy because dominant teams are capable of playing explosive, big games; and any weak team can get killed, even by another weak team.

By sticking to the good and average teams, if your underdog plays great, they will win the game outright. If they play decent football and stay close in the turnover battle, they can cover the spread in a close 3- or 4-point game. You will only usually lose if they don't show up and don't play competitive ball. What really makes my strategy work is this: If you are betting against a team with an average offense that finds it tough to score more than 20 points, you are in great position. All your team has to do is score between 13-16 points and you can cover the spread. Most offenses in the NFL are not dominant enough to cover big point spreads on a consistent basis. Of course, you won't bet every game that falls into these categories, only the games that you like.

You may be wondering, "How often during an NFL season am I going to find similar caliber teams playing with a 6 to 9 point spread?" You might be surprised to know that this type of game comes up about once a week, if not more often.

Here are a few examples from the 2004 NFL season.

1) NFL WEEK 16 2004 NEW YORK GIANTS AT CINCINNATI. NEW YORK GIANTS +6

Coming into this game, I classified both teams as average, Group 3, teams. The Bengals had one more win than the Giants because the Giants were building for the future and playing rookie quarterback Eli Manning. I usually don't like betting on rookie quarterbacks, but Manning was coming on: He and the Giants had played great at home the week before against the best team in the league, Pittsburgh, barely losing in a close contest, 33 to 30. The spread was +6 for this week because the Giants had lost seven games in a row coming in. I don't like betting on cold teams, but I thought the Giants had just played well and Manning was progressing well, not looking like a rookie anymore. To me, that was key.

Cincinnati in 2004 was an inconsistent, average team. I thought the spread was too high and should have been 3 1/2 to 4 points. But remember, I don't bet the spread, I bet the game. I didn't like the game because I thought the spread was off; I liked it because I thought the Giants could easily cover the spread, or even win the game.

The Giants played great, driving easily on the Bengals' defense. Cincinnati won a close game at the end, 23-22, with a final comeback drive, but the Giants covered the spread.

2) NFL WEEK 17 2004 NEW ORLEANS AT CAROLINA. NEW ORLEANS +7

I classified both teams Group 3 average teams, yet they were close to being in Group 2. Heading into this game, they had similar stories. Both teams had terrible starts to the season. Carolina actually started at 1-7. Both teams had been written off early in the year, but had great finishes to the season. Heading into the game, both teams had a record of 7-8, and the winner had a chance of grabbing a wildcard spot, depending on how St. Louis and Minnesota fared in their games. New Orleans had won three games in a row, and their defense, at one point the worst in the league, was playing well. The way I saw this game, either team could win it.

Carolina had the home field advantage, and got respect because they were the NFC Champs. However, I knew not to worry about past-season results. Carolina was heavily favored for no real apparent reason to me.

New Orleans actually played great and won the game outright, 21-18.

3) NFL 1ST ROUND PLAYOFFS 2005. NEW YORK JETS AT SAN DIEGO. NEW YORK JETS +7

In the 2005 NFL playoffs, the Chargers played at home as 7-point favorites against the Jets. That spread was too big. You could make a point that the Jets were a better team than the Chargers and I liked two main things about taking the Jets. The first was that the Jets had a great defense, among the top three in the league, so if the Jets scored 13-20 points, they probably would cover the spread. The second thing I liked was that Chad Pennington is a quarterback that almost never made mistakes; he gave a consistent performance each week. I bought 1/2 point and got a line on the Jets of +7 1/2 and -120. The Jets won the game outright in a close battle.

Betting on an equal or better team with 6 to 9 points in your pocket is just one strategy you can use in football. It's best to wait until Week 4 or 5 of the season to use this strategy, because it takes that long for you to get a feel for the quality of teams.

2. NFL OVER/UNDER WAGERS

When betting on over/unders, you are betting more on the flow of the game and the scoring power of both teams than the defense. When betting on teams, the turnover factor is much more of an issue than it is in over/under wagers. Here are a few good tips that will help you find good NFL over/under wagers.

First, let's discuss the flow of an NFL game. The flow of a game is often dictated by the score. If the score in a given NFL game is 3-0 at the end of the first quarter, that score will help the next quarter to be low scoring, because the two teams tend to continue playing conservatively. If the score after the first quarter is 14-0, it will help the next quarter to go over because the losing team will be passing more to try to get back into the game. Quite simply, low-scoring games involve a lot more rushing, while high scoring games involve more passing. Most NFL coaches are conservative and will punt the ball in a close game. They are often unwilling to make big mistakes or take big gambles.

BET GAMES, NOT SPREADS

My first tip is that you should bet the game, not the spread. If you see two high-scoring teams playing each other with a spread of 48 or 49, betting the under may not be such a good move. Two great offenses can easily score 24 or 25 points each in an NFL game, or even 35 points each, as both offenses will be trying to exceed the other team's scores. Bettors are sometimes afraid to bet over 48, but it can be a good move with the right game. A lot of high spreads end up going over because Vegas and the bookmakers cannot set a line high enough for two great offenses.

THE QUARTERBACK FACTOR

When contemplating over/unders, analyze the quarterbacks because they are key to any over/under bet. The difference in whether a game goes over or under the spread often comes down to whether teams are able to get touchdowns or field goals on their drives. The 4-point difference between a touchdown and a field goal is huge. Great quarterbacks and great offenses are able to turn drives into touchdowns, while mediocre quarterbacks and offenses settle for field goals. For the most part, look for overs with good and great quarterbacks; look for unders with average quarterbacks.

THE COACHING FACTOR

Coaching decisions on down situations also make a huge impact on a game's total. If a coach has only one or two to go on fourth down when his team is at the opposing 30-40 yard line, what he decides to do will make a big impact on the outcome of the game. If he punts, no points are scored and the other team is backed up. If he goes for it and converts, it will often lead to 3 or 7 points. Even if his team fails to convert, the other team will have good field position going the other way. If he goes for the field goal, there is about a 55 to 60 percent chance that the kicker will make it from that distance and add 3 points to the score.

Know your coaches. Regardless of the spread, if you bet the over, you want your coach to have an offensive mindset. If you bet the under, you want him to have a defensive mindset. Getting to know the coaches is simple: Review play-by-play of past games on the Internet to see what they do on fourth downs.

Teams that love to throw the deep ball will help a game go over when they connect for quick, big plays. Even when they miss, the clock stops, and that's also good for the over. Teams that consistently run the ball help unders a great deal. If you have the under and a team scores 7 points on an 11-minute drive, that is okay because the drive ate up a lot of clock. Their next drive could be six minutes long and result in no points. Read between the stats: How *quickly* a team scores can be as important as how much they score.

LEAVING ROOM FOR ERROR

My next tip is to leave room for error. I will almost never bet any game under 37 points. I want room for error with all of my bets. Any two teams in the league are capable of scoring 20 points each on any given Sunday. By betting a game under 37, you are asking for a 17-14 type of game. You're just looking to squeeze by. Never look to squeeze by with your wagers, look to cover your spreads as easily as possible. Betting under 37 leaves little room for error. The only time I would recommend the bet is when weather conditions are disastrous, with a big snowstorm or constant, heavy rainfall.

THE WEATHER FACTOR

In betting over/unders, weather is a touchy subject. People often ask whether bad weather really helps a game go under. (And obviously, domes allow for more scoring.) In outdoor stadiums, snowfall during a game or a little bit of rain doesn't ensure a low scoring, grind-it-out game. Weather helps games go under during extreme weather, such as a total snowstorm the entire game, constant rain, and heavy winds. Extreme conditions make it tough to pass and catch and hard to maintain footing, so offenses cannot move. High winds will hurt a team's potential to make big plays in the passing game and it will lead teams to run more, which translates to less scoring.

Keep an eye open for weather forecasts, and if disastrous weather is predicted, the under can be a great pick with two average offenses—though I'd be careful with two great offenses. In 2004, Pittsburgh beat Miami 13-3 in Week 3 in what I called the "Sog Bowl." The game was played while Hurricane Jeanne hit South Florida. There was constant, heavy rain and the field was flooded with water for almost the entire game. No one could pass the ball consistently.

Also, consider taking the points on heavy underdogs in weather-disaster games. The weather will diminish the talent capabilities of the better team and will make the game more of an equal battle between eleven men versus eleven men. The main factor in crazy weather games is for a team to limit its mistakes. On November 28, 2004, the 11-point underdog, Oakland, upset Denver in Colorado in a blizzard. The weather made it anyone's game because there were so many variables. Watching the game, you knew that you could throw the point spread out the window. It looked like a Pee Wee game with all the mistakes: poor passes, fumbles, players slipping. Even great players look average in disaster weather!

BEWARE PREVIOUS STATS
I also suggest that you give no credit to previous stats such as, "In September, 57 percent of games go under." That means nothing. Analyze each game's over/under on its own merits.

Look at what happened if the teams have played against each other earlier in the season. What went right? What went wrong? Was it a low-scoring running game? Was it a high-scoring passing game? Do you think the upcoming game will be a repeat of their last match, or was their last match an aberration? Don't analyze the last time they played if it didn't happen in the current season. Teams change considerably every year, with personnel changes as well as coaching changes.

LOOK AT PREVIOUS GAMES

My final piece of advice is that a team's score often is similar to their last few games. Some teams keep pumping big points each week, while others struggle. Bet the over on consistent offenses, and the under on mediocre offenses. Either an offense is going well or it's mediocre; either the defense is playing well or it's mediocre. Teams don't change overnight. Teams sometimes experience a negative change or an improvement, but they generally hold true to form. Unlike the NBA, NHL, or even MLB, there are almost no trades during a season in the NFL. Teams will play to their style and to their scoring potential fairly consistently during the entire season.

GOOD ADVICE

In betting over/unders in the NFL, if you are unsure about a wager, don't be afraid to stand pat. Don't over-analyze things, either: You either think that an offense will be able to score effectively on a defense, or you think they will not, period.

3. NFL GAMES ARE HIGHER SCORING WHEN THE GAME IS PLAYED IN A DOME

For the most part, NFL games are higher scoring in domes than on grass. The fact that the game is being played in a dome is factored into the total that Vegas puts up, but it often is not given enough weight. For example, if you had bet the over in every game played in domes during the 2003 NFL season, you would have done pretty well. The average score in a dome game in the NFL in 2003 was a whopping 45 1/2 points per game, a lot higher than the average scored on grass.

You might think that a lot of NFL teams play in domes, but only six teams do (although the Dallas Cowboys play in a stadium that is similar to a dome, with artificial turf). The dome teams are the Atlanta Falcons, New Orleans Saints, St. Louis Rams, Detroit Lions, Minnesota Vikings and Indianapolis Colts. Many dome teams build their offenses around the fact that they play indoors with high-powered passing attacks.

What makes a game played in a dome more likely to be high scoring than a game that is played outdoors? Here are ten factors:

1. No wind helps quarterbacks pass.
2. Receivers are faster on turf, and run better routes.
3. Running backs have more traction to assist in longer and consistent runs.
4. No rain, snow or cold helps quarterbacks throw the ball better.
5. No rain, snow or cold helps receivers catch the ball.
6. There is no swirling wind to affect kickers.
7. Kickers are not affected by rain or snow, thus allowing for a smooth kick.
8. Regular temperature helps players play without any distractions.
9. Receivers can catch the ball more easily; when it's cold, the ball feels like a rock

10. Players are overall more athletic and free when they aren't affected by bad weather

When analyzing a game, take the weather forecast into account. You also may find that a game's over/under spread is based primarily on where the game is played. For example, a game that is being played on a snowy day in Buffalo may lead to a low spread of 34 1/2. Consider taking the over if the weather clears up before game time. Based on the weather forecast, the spread may have dropped too low, and it might not snow after all during the game. Maybe it will simply be very cold that day. A team can score plenty of points on a cold day in the NFL if it isn't windy. Obviously, the less wind the better it is for a team's passing game.

Before making the wager, check the local weather forecast on the Internet. I recommend weather.com, which gives a full breakdown of the weather and has forecasts for each NFL stadium during game times, with complete temperature and wind breakdown. Of course, the closer it is to kickoff, the more accurate the forecast will be. I recommend waiting until close to kickoff to make your wager. If you find that it will be a cold day, but the field will be clear with very little wind, look at betting the over if both offenses are capable.

4. TURNOVERS GIVE WAGERS ADDED UN-PREDICTABILITY

Football is the most popular sport to bet on in North America, however, as I previously stated, what makes it tough to wager on is the turnover factor. Turnovers rear their ugly heads and make good teams look bad and bad teams look good. They can make overs go under, and under bets go over. A turnover in football has much more impact than in basketball, because in football, a 94-yard interception return for a touchdown, or a 75-yard fumble return for a touchdown is a 10 to 14-point swing. "How often does that happen?" you may wonder. More than you might think, at least a few times every NFL Sunday.

In basketball, if one team throws the ball away and the other team takes that turnover and turns it into a basket, it can easily be made up with a couple of good plays. But in football, those 10 to 14-point swings are often the difference in the game. So, beware the turnover factor in football when placing your wagers as a turnover can make or break your bet. A couple of key misplays can make a good bet go bad, even if your team has outplayed its opponent.

The better team does not always win.

5. BET AGAINST YOUNG OR UNPROVEN BACKUP QUARTERBACKS

The quarterback is the most important position in football and he is the player that can often make or break your bet. As the season progresses, teams often go through a transition period with their quarterbacks. A starting quarterback might get injured and a backup comes in and proves to be incompetent. Because of free agency and the salary cap, very few NFL teams have two quality quarterbacks on their roster. Some backup quarterbacks are weak and if you know who they are, you can make money wagering against them. For example, some backup quarterbacks come into the game, cannot read the defense, and simply cannot make plays. They actually help the other team's offense by giving them good field position from a lot of three and outs.

In the 2003 NFL season, the Atlanta Falcons were an up and coming team, coming off a big playoff win the previous year in Green Bay. Atlanta's star quarterback, Michael Vick, got injured in the pre-season and backup Doug Johnson came in as their starter in his absence. Doug had played one game the previous year and had played well, beating the New York Giants—but that was just one game. After a few games, Johnson's poor play noticeably hurt the team. If you had started betting against the Falcons in the spread for their first eleven games of the season, you would have made good money. They only covered the spread in one of their first seven games, and in only four of their first eleven games. When Vick came back from injury, the Falcons won three of four games with him starting, covering the spread in three of them. Doug Johnson had one of the worst quarterback ratings of any starter in the NFL in the 2003 season—money was there to be made by betting against him.

Most rookie quarterbacks sink before they swim and betting against them can be a profitable way to make money in the NFL, but if you see a rookie quarterback playing consistently well, don't bet against him. For example, Ben Roethlisberger won his first 14 games as a rookie in 2004 as a starter, but he was a unique exception. You won't see that kind of rookie quarterback success happen again for a long time. Roethlisberger probably had the best season ever by an NFL rookie quarterback.

Sometimes a team that is already out of playoff contention will decide to start playing their young, first-round draft pick quarterback. The rookie will often struggle. Once you see that he is struggling, you might have a good bet against the young quarterback in continuous games, at least until he proves you wrong.

However, some backup quarterbacks are pretty good. They may be players who have had solid seasons as a starter in the past, but have had to move on to a different team because they lost their starting position to an up and coming quarterback. For example, Alexander Wright came in for injured quarterback Kyle Boller in 2003 and played great ball for Baltimore. He helped them win five of their last seven games. But Wright had experience as a quarterback, as he had been a starter earlier in his career.

Since head coaches announce their starting quarterbacks a few days before each game, you are able to bet against young or backup quarterbacks who are unproven NFL players. Even though the spread is affected by who is starting, often you can find a weak quarterback playing at home as a 1 1/2 to 3 point favorite or a 1 1/2 to 3 point underdog against an equally talented team. Often, the weak quarterback's team will get killed by 20 to 25 points, and you can easily win your wager.

Spot the weak quarterbacks and bet against them in the right situations.

6. BET ON QUALITY QUARTERBACKS

On the other hand, I suggest betting on quality quarterbacks. Football is so close when you factor in the point spread that more often than not the quarterback will make the difference between winning and losing. If you like a football wager, you still should ask yourself these questions before placing your wager.

1. Does this team have a quality quarterback?
2. Is this quarterback consistent?
3. Can this quarterback turn clutch drives into points when the game is on the line?

4. Can I trust this quarterback not to make stupid decisions and throw bad interceptions?

If the answer is yes to all these questions, go ahead and place your bet with confidence. Sometimes you might wager on a team +4 points, and your quarterback may be driving downfield with two minutes left, losing by 7 points. Will he be able to make clutch plays in a two-minute offense to help his team tie the game? Or will he throw an interception or turn the ball over on downs? Never forget that clutch quarterbacks and smart quarterbacks will make you money in close games!

This statement may sound basic, but bettors often forget the simple things and get distracted by the complex things. If you bet on good quarterbacks, you will be in position to win a lot of your bets. If you had bet on Tom Brady on the money line in his first ten NFL playoff games, you would be 10 and 0. It is not a coincidence that he won: Bet on good, consistent quarterbacks.

You might think that everything, including the quarterback, is factored into the spread already. However, as I stated earlier, in all sports, the team that wins the game will cover the spread more times than not. All underdogs automatically cover the spread, and favorites that win cover the spread more times than they don't. Sometimes you have to think in a simpler fashion, and just bet on great players or great teams. You can be successful at it, too!

7. WAGERING ON NFL ROAD TEAMS

When taking a road team to cover a spread in the NFL, consider two factors. First, if you're going to take a road team as a favorite to cover the spread, then you should believe that the road team has the following qualities:

1. They are a superior team
2. They have a better quarterback
3. The team is hotter
4. The visiting team has more talent than the home team

If the road team doesn't meet these criteria, your bet often is just a toss up in a close game, where either team can win based on who makes the big play at the end of the game. When I take a road team as a favorite in any sport, it is usually because I think it has more talent and plays at a different level than the home team.

My second point is that if you take a road favorite, buy points to get the road favorite at -2 1/2. Why? Because NFL road teams often sneak away with a 3-point victory, even if they are a much better team than the home team. Here's an example of a solid NFL road-team bet: In Week 4 of the 2004 NFL season, there were two great road teams to bet on: The New England Patriots were 5-point favorites in Buffalo, and the St. Louis Rams were 3 1/2 point favorites in San Francisco. In both cases, I bet on the road team, but I bought points and sacrificed some of the money line to make each pick at -2 1/2. I ended up getting New England at -2 1/2 and -160, and St. Louis at -2 1/2 and -130. I believed that I was betting on superior and more talented teams.

New England had won 17 straight NFL games heading into the game, and looked great at 3-0 on the season thus far. On the other hand, Buffalo was 0-3 and looked terrible; their offense could not score. I knew that I had the vastly better team and Buffalo would have to beat a team that had won 17 in a row. I figured that the only way Buffalo could win the game would be if some crazy, unexpected turnovers occurred. Sure enough, New England won by 14.

In the other game, San Francisco was 0-3 and looked terrible the previous week, losing 34-0 in Seattle. St. Louis was still a great offensive team and they were 1-2 coming in, but I thought that they were better than their record indicated. St. Louis jumped out to a 24-0 lead and won the game 24-14.

In both cases, I took a superior road team and I won.

A lot of 3- or 4-point spreads in the NFL involve teams that play at the same level, so be careful betting the road team in these situations. For example, in the same week as my Rams and Patriots wagers, Tennessee was in San Diego favored by 3 points. A lot of people bet on Tennessee, but it was a terrible pick for two reasons:

They were not a far superior team to San Diego. They might have been better, but by no means were they far superior. (Both teams were 1 and 2 coming in.)

The previous season's MVP, quarterback Steve McNair, was injured and would not play. Never bet on a team when their best player is out, especially since the quarterback is so important.

I didn't touch that game. San Diego blew Tennessee out of the water.

8. NFL INJURIES

Taking advantage of injuries in the NFL is a way that you can make money in sports gambling. However, in the NFL, it is sometimes tricky to figure out if a player is playing or not. Injured players are given a status report that can change daily, from Wednesday to Sunday, based on their improvement. The levels of status are listed below and their official chances of playing, according to their team's report.

1. Probable	75 percent
2. Questionable	50 percent
3. Doubtful	25 percent
4. Out	0 percent
5. Injured Reserve	Out for the season

None of these injury levels guarantees that a player will or will not play. Players often play a lot higher percentage of games than what their listed status suggests, so be careful. At the same time, injury reports can help when you are deciding whether to bet on individual games, division winners, and other future bets. The closer a player's listed status gets to Sunday, the more accurate it becomes. Often, you will see a player listed as doubtful, which suggests he probably won't play, but doubtful players actually play quite often. If their status is probable, then most likely they will play unless they have a drastic change with their injury before game time.

The main position to follow, of course, is the quarterback. Quarterback status is easy to follow because head coaches announce who will be starting, usually 24 to 72 hours before the game, as they have to prepare the starter in practice. Focus on the quarterbacks that are out and consider betting against the team that is playing a backup quarterback. Impact players can be found at many different positions in the NFL, so look for teams that are missing their impact players, regardless of position, keeping in mind that the quarterback position is the most important. If one non-quarterback player is out, it may not make a big difference, as there may be good backup players at different positions who can fill in adequately.

You want to bet against NFL teams that are decimated by injuries; that is, four to nine key players or starters are out of the lineup. One non-quarterback player is tough to equate into a betting advantage, but if a bunch of starters are out, a domino effect may kick in and cripple a team.

For instance, in the 2004 NFL season, the majority of the defensive starters for the Tennessee Titans were injured for the last few games of the season. The Titans were playing almost all backups. So many defensive players were injured that five of their final six games easily went over the over/under total because their defense had collapsed.

Follow the league carefully and determine which teams are being seriously affected by injuries. If you want to know for sure whether a certain player will be playing, watch *NFL Gameday*. During the show, the analysts usually mention the status of questionable players. Look to take advantage with the right game with the right players missing.

CHAPTER 14

3 TOP TIPS FOR BETTING BASEBALL

1. NEVER A LOCK IN BASEBALL

More than in the other three major North American team sports, anything can happen in baseball. In basketball, when a player shoots the ball, he wants it to go into the hoop. In football, when a quarterback throws the ball, he aims it towards a receiver's hands. In hockey, when a player shoots the puck, he aims it towards the goalie. But in baseball, players just want to hit the ball hard and do not have full control over where the ball is going! Hitting a baseball is the hardest thing to do in all four major sports. Sometimes a team can hit the ball really hard all night, but it goes right into the opposing team's defense.

The unpredictability of hitting the ball often leaves superstars without results while role players shine. Unlike other sports where you can find some pretty safe bets, the element of doubt is always present in baseball. Look at it this way: Would you be shocked if David Wright batted 0-4 with one strikeout and one pop out? Probably not; he just happened to have an off day. However, you would be shocked if Tim Duncan shot 1-18 from the field in basketball.

Also, home field advantage does not mean as much in baseball as it does in other sports.

Betting on baseball can be good when you can find hot or cold pitchers, or hot or cold teams. However, never look at any baseball game and think that you have found a lock! During the summer, when the only major sport to bet on is baseball, you might want to take the whole summer off and wait for the NFL in September if you find that you are not successful betting baseball. Due to the unpredictability, I would not recommend risking a large size of your bankroll on any one given wager when you bet baseball.

2. WAGER ON HOT PITCHERS

The starting pitcher is a very important factor in whether or not you are going to win your wager in major league baseball. "Good pitching will beat good hitting" is a common axiom in baseball. As in most sports, a good defense can slow down or stop a good offense. For example, let's review Game 6 of the 2003 World Series with Florida against the New York Yankees. With the highest payroll in baseball and a stacked lineup from one to nine, the Yankees could not muster a single run against the dominating pitching of Josh Beckett. So often, if you can find a hot starting pitcher to bet on, all you need is your team to score three or four runs and you will win your wager.

Baseball is a sport in which any team can beat another team on any given day. You will get very nice money lines to work with, even when you find a hot pitcher. Lines like -135 and -160 are commonplace. Why is betting on a hot pitcher a good wager to make? Most pitchers go on hot and cold streaks during the season. When a pitcher is pitching well, it seems to carry over to his next start. Below are a few more reasons why betting on a hot pitcher can be a good move.

A) CONFIDENCE
When a pitcher is pitching well, he throws his pitches with more confidence, which allows for greater success.

B) HEALTH
When a pitcher is pitching well, it is because he is at full body strength. His arm is feeling fresh, he doesn't have any minor injuries, and he feels good about his health.

C) CONTROL
When a pitcher is pitching well, he has control over the location of his pitches, which are in a groove. He feels a consistent flow and can pinpoint his pitches.

D) DEFENSE
When a pitcher is playing well, he often is playing ahead of a solid defense that is making big plays and committing few errors.

When a pitcher is pitching poorly, just the opposite occurs: he has no confidence, he might be slightly hurt, he has no control of his pitches, and the defense may be weak. For instance, Roy Halladay won the AL Cy Young award for best pitcher in the American League in the 2003 MLB season. However, he was not a consistent pitcher all year long; he had some ups and downs.

In April, Halladay recorded no wins, yet he was still able to finish with 22 wins on the year! He got off to a slow start and would not have been a good wager in an individual game early. However, once April was over, he won his next 11 starts: amazing! Halladay also was dominating in September, recording a couple of complete game shutouts, giving up very few runs, and winning five games. When he was hot, the money line was not as good as when he was cold. However, he was still a good wager. Why? Because it is better to bet on a hot pitcher at -195 who wins, then bet on a cold pitcher at +120 who ends up losing. Halladay was a perfect example of a Cy Young pitcher who experienced hot and cold streaks during the season.

The key is checking the pitcher's last three games to see how he fared. If a pitcher is hot, there's a good chance that he will continue to pitch well in his next start. Pitchers usually don't win one decision and then lose the next one, going back and forth and finishing 14-13. They go on streaks. You can get good, hot pitchers with decent money lines of -130 to -175, not bad at all!

It may occasionally be worthwhile to wager on hot pitchers -1 1/2 runs in order to get a better money line. But only do this with a very hot pitcher who has good bats behind him for run support. If you are going to wager on a team at -1 1/2 runs in order to get a better money line, only do it with road teams. That way, you will ensure that you get all nine innings for your team to get runs. If you pick a home team, they could be up by one run and not get their final at-bat in the ninth, causing you to lose your wager at -1 1/2. And in the event that the game goes to extra innings, the home team usually wins by one run, unless they hit a multi-run home run.

One final thing to remember is that in baseball, you do not need to be overly concerned about taking a road team over a home team. Some teams even finish the season of 162 games with a better road record than at home. Check the standings to see how teams play at home and on the road. An emotional crowd cannot heavily sway the game to the extent that it sometimes does in basketball. Some of the best bets are hot pitchers on the road in baseball with a good money line.

Overall, you are better off betting on home teams in baseball, but if you find a hot team with a hot pitcher on the road, betting the road team should not worry you.

3. BASEBALL OFFERS GOOD OPPORTUNITIES TO WAGER THE OVER

As in any line in sports gambling, the over/under in a baseball game is designed to attract equal wagering from both sides. You can take advantage of the over when you find that two poor, cold or young pitchers are starting a game. Betting the over can be a good bet for many reasons. Sometimes the oddsmakers cannot set the line high enough when two poor pitchers are playing each other. For example, they can't make the spread 14 1/2 or higher; if they did, people would bet on the under and hope the teams didn't score. Often you will find two poor pitchers facing each other with a spread of 10 1/2, 9 1/2, 9 or even lower. Look for these situations and bet them over.

Another reason you can be successful with this approach is because when two poor starting pitchers face each other, their managers will be quick to give them the hook if the game looks like it's getting out of hand. Once the starting pitchers leave the game, the middle relief pitchers, the worst pitchers in the majors, come into the game. It is not unusual to then see an avalanche of runs pour in.

I like betting overs in baseball games because, unlike the other three major sports, time is not a factor. You are not betting against the clock, you are betting against the poor pitching staffs that are forced to get three outs on the other team before their half of the inning is over. In the three other major sports, a lot of clock can tick off during the drought phase of a game, and a losing team cannot catch up. In baseball there is always the chance for a big inning.

I once bet on the Toronto Blue Jays, for example, and they were winning by seven runs headed into the bottom of the ninth inning. The Angels miraculously scored seven runs in the ninth, and came back to win the game in the tenth inning. Of course, I lost my wager. On a different day, I wagered the over at 11 due to two poor pitchers. The game was scoreless after six innings; however, in the seventh inning, each team erupted for 5 runs. Then, in the eighth inning, I got two more runs to win my bet.

The key with betting overs is to find games in which two really cold pitchers are facing one another. With between 80 to 100 games played each week in MLB, these games aren't hard to find. Take advantage of the Internet to research the stats online and look at the last three starts by the pitchers. If the pitchers had poor outings, chances are good that their next outing will also be poor.

Don't be afraid to bet 9, 9 1/2 or 10 over. When you check the final scores for the day, you often will see a lot of 10-8 scores or 9-4 scores or even 13-10 scores. If you check who the starting pitchers were in these games, you will notice that they were weak pitchers who had been on a cold streak.

Also check the game preview half an hour before each game at the major sports websites, where you will find the starting line-ups for each team. If a few major offensive players are out of the lineup, consider that factor when making your over/under wagers.

Here is a method you can use in finding the good over possibilities. Look for opposing pitchers with an ERA of 5 or more who have had poor starts in their last three outings. Then look at baseball stats on the Internet and pull up team rankings in the runs column. Runs are true indicators of how good an offense is. Analyze the teams' recent offensive production and their run production all year to see if the offenses have been playing well recently. If they have and if you like the spread, consider taking the over in the game. Be selective. Remember that you can find these kinds of games several times a week, so only bet the good ones.

Bet with confidence in baseball, but not overconfidence. In other words, keep your best within the money management guidelines we've discussed.

CHAPTER

15

7 TOP TIPS FOR BETTING BASKETBALL

I consider basketball to have the best betting opportunities among the four major sports. Compared to other sports, basketball has fewer variables that can disrupt a good wager. In football, the big turnover is a variable that can make or break you. In hockey, a team can outshoot its opponent 40 to 20 but lose 2-0 because of hot goaltending. In baseball, the players can hit the ball well, but those drives can get caught. In basketball each possession has about the same value—1, 2, or 3 points. And one play will not kill your bet, as it can in the other sports.

1. WATCH OUT FOR NBA TEAMS PLAYING TWO GAMES IN TWO NIGHTS

The statistics prove that an NBA team playing in back-to-back games against a team that had the previous night off will be at a disadvantage. They are often physically fatigued and sometimes they are not mentally up for the second game. The good news for you as a bettor is that this disadvantage is not always represented in the spread.

Look for spreads in which a fresh home team is playing a road team that played the previous night. You should not base your entire betting strategy on this point, of course, but it is a factor when making your picks.

2. FIND VALUE WITH INJURIES IN BASKETBALL

Very few players anymore play all 82 games in an NBA season. You often will find that key players rest for a game or two due to some minor injuries, or they may even be out for two or three weeks with a major injury. A great opportunity occurs when, before the line moves, you discover that a player isn't playing. The point spread will be affected by a player's injuries, but it often is not affected by more than a couple of points.

You might obtain this information from the Internet or sports tickers on television and satellite, which can be key in these situations, because games are scheduled for, let's say, 7:30 p.m., but do not start until 7:40 p.m. Keep in mind that all basketball games start 10 minutes after the scheduled time listed in the paper. During those 10 minutes, you can watch the pregame tip-off information that the play-by-play crew gives, and they will tell you who is a scratch. Once you get the information, you usually have five minutes to place your wager.

For the best injury reports on the web, go to covers.com, which not only tells you who is injured, but when the player probably will be coming back. Covers.com updates its injury information regularly. I always glance at injury reports before making all wagers. You also can use CBSsportsline.com and click on the players' link, where you can read a bit of a fantasy/injury report on each player.

It is important for you to realize how great an impact the injured player makes and ask yourself some key questions. How important is he? Is there a player off the bench that can fill his role and match his production? Will he affect the team's offense or defense or both? How has his team fared in recent games when he has not played?

Here is one situation where I benefited from an injury report. During the final day of regular season games in the 2002-2003 NBA season, the Dallas Mavericks were on the road facing the San Antonio Spurs. The point spread opened up with the Spurs at -3 1/2 points. The Spurs had already clinched home court advantage throughout the NBA playoffs with the best record in the league, so they had nothing to play for. But winning was important to Dallas. If they won this game, they would still have the third seed in the West playoffs, but they would earn home-court advantage against the Sacramento Kings, their probable second-round opponent. Knowing this, I still wasn't convinced that I should take Dallas, because San Antonio at home could outplay them with their stronger, taller, more physical team.

However, ninety minutes before tip-off, the local sports ticker announced that Tim Duncan, the MVP of the league had been put on the injured list for San Antonio. He would not play and neither would the team's second-leading scorer, Stephen Jackson. I knew right away that San Antonio was throwing in the towel for the game by resting their key players. I also felt that they could not win without them. I immediately wagered money on Dallas while I could still get a good spread of +2 points. Dallas easily won the game by 21 points.

These situations occur during the regular season quite often, maybe not to the extent of this bet, but they do come up on a regular basis. Try to gather as much information as possible before making the wager based on certain players not playing. For example, check previous box scores to see how the team did when that player was out, so that you can get a feel for his impact.

In addition to injured players, also look for suspended players. In the 2003-2004 NBA season, Tim Duncan accidentally pushed an official, and he was automatically suspended for the next game against the Clippers. The spread going into the game was still San Antonio at -4 1/2 points. However, the Clippers won the game 91-83. During the same season, Shaq went on a verbal tirade about the officials after a game in Toronto. He was suspended for the next game against Indiana, and the Lakers got creamed by over 20 points.

A lot of sports gambling comes down to timing: The quicker you can get information, the better off you will be. For example, if you find out that a key player has thrown a punch or pushed an official, you know that he will miss the team's next game. You can often get a wager in before the announcement of a suspension is made, and get a nice edge on the bet. If you were wrong about the suspension, you can always bet against your original bet and eat the juice.

Below, I have listed key players in the NBA whose team largely relies on them for victories. This list is based not only on talent but more so on their ability to help their team win. This information is current as of July 2008, so if players are on different teams when you refer to the list, their value to a team may not be the same. I made two lists. List "A" is for great bets, "B" is for good bets. The players are not ranked in any specific order.

A: GREAT BETS

Tim Duncan (San Antonio Spurs)
Tracy McGrady (Houston Rockets)
Yao Ming (Houston Rockets)
Kevin Garnett (Boston Celtics)
Lebron James (Cleveland Cavaliers)
Dwayne Wade (Miami Heat)
Baron Davis (Los Angles Clippers)
Kobe Bryant (Los Angles Lakers)
Steve Nash (Phoenix Suns)
Amare Stoudemire (Phoenix Suns)
Chris Paul (New Orleans Hornets)
Dwight Howard (Orlando Magic)
Joe Johnson (Atlanta Hawks)
Ron Artest (Sacramento Kings)
Allen Iverson (Denver Nuggets)
Carmelo Anthony (Denver Nuggets)
Deron Williams (Utah Jazz)
Elton Brand (Philadelphia 76ers)
Dirk Nowitzki (Dallas Mavericks)

B: GOOD BETS

Paul Pierce (Boston Celtics)
Marcus Camby (Los Angles Clippers)
Chris Bosh (Toronto Raptors)
Michael Redd (Milwaukee Bucks)
Brandon Roy (Portland Trailblazers)
Gilbert Arenas (Washington Wizards)
Hedo Turkoglu (Orlando Magic)
Vince Carter (New Jersey Nets)
Antawn Jamison (Washington Wizards)
Kevin Durant (Seattle Supersonics)
Stephen Jackson (Golden State Warriors)

You might be thinking, "What about Tony Parker or Carlos Boozer or other great players?" Well, right now the Spurs have enough talent to still win games without Parker, and the Jazz have good team play even without Carlos Boozer. The A list is the great list: When these players are out, the team will really be affected. When the spreads come out and you know these players are not playing, look to see if the spread is still good enough to bet against the shorthanded team—and vice versa. Even if you can get a money line of -400, but you know that Lebron James will not be playing—depending on who and where they are playing—a good move can be making the -400 money line wager, because you know that without Lebron James, Cleveland will struggle immensely.

If Vegas has overcompensated the spread due to an injured player and you see someone off the bench who can step into that player's minutes and play well, then you can bet on the injured team by taking some extra points. Check previous games when this player has been out to see if the team still played up to par or not, and find out who took most of his minutes. Use this information in part to help decide if and how much to wager.

When an NBA team goes on the road with their best player injured, I know the team will struggle, so I like to bet against them on the money line. The effect is less at home, but the team often struggles when they go on the road. Betting against road teams that are competing without their best player is almost always a good move if you can get a good spread or money line. Actually, when an NBA team is missing its best player, I rarely bet on them. I may not bet against them, but I will not bet on a shorthanded team regardless of the spread. A shorthanded team is more likely to get blown out.

In conclusion, a great team without its best player usually turns into an average or below average team. Take advantage with the right game when a team is shorthanded.

College basketball also can be a great opportunity for taking advantage of shorthanded players. In the NBA, there is often a quality backup ready to fill in and show off his talents, but in college ball, a great player usually cannot be replaced by anyone off the bench. Some teams in college just collapse when their key player is injured. Patiently look for these situations.

In any sport you must consider these points when looking at a player's value to a spread or game.

- How key is the player?
- Can this player be adequately replaced by the backup on the team?
- Does he affect their offense, defense, or both?
- How has the team fared in the past without this player?

Stay informed about injured or suspended players. Remember to be cautious in your wagers, however, because backups can step up and play well in a game. In the long run, you can show a handsome profit betting against shorthanded teams.

3. TAKE ADVANTAGE OF INCOMPLETE ROSTERS AND TRAVEL SCHEDULES IN THE PRESEASON

You might wonder, "How could I bet on the NBA preseason?" I used to think like that too. Why would I wager on a game in which neither team really cares whether they win—and the best players may not even be in the game during crunch time?

However, there is money to be made by betting on preseason basketball.

In basketball, whoever is on the court is still going to give a great effort, if not close to a maximum effort. The main difference in effort will be in the intensity level of the players. If Kevin Garnett is on the floor, he is still Kevin Garnett, and he will help you win your bet. So, if you can bet against a team that is resting key players, you will have a good chance of winning your wager.

Always look to bet against teams with no depth, because those teams will not be able to compensate for the absence of one or two players. Actually, a lot of coaches give big minutes to their starters in the preseason, usually about 30 to 40 minutes each, because they want to get their starters in game shape. By analyzing minutes in box scores, you can discover which coaches give their star players the most playing time in the preseason.

Use the Internet, television and any other source you have to find out if certain players will be resting.

The second way to win money in preseason basketball is betting against teams that have played the night before. This rule of two games in two nights works in the preseason and the regular season. Reviewing the statistics for the 2004-2005 NBA preseason, if you had just blindly bet on the team that had not played the night before against a team that had played the night before, you would have done very well for yourself. In your first 22 bets, you would have gone 18 and 4, an amazing winning record of over 81 percent. Here is a list of reasons why betting against teams playing back-to-back games in the preseason can be a good bet.

A coach will be more prone to rest key players in the second night of back-to-back games.

Players in the preseason are not always in the best shape yet. When they play two games in two nights, they may not give the same effort in their second game.

If a coach still dresses everyone in a back-to-back game, he is more likely to spread around the playing time, giving bench players more minutes—and you more opportunity to win by betting against the tired and weak team.

The oddsmakers don't make teams big favorites in the pre-season, so you can often take a much better team at -1 1/2 or 2 points.

Whenever you can bet against a team that doesn't care whether they win or lose, or is resting players, you have an advantage, preseason or regular season.

One warning: There are no locks in the preseason. A coach may change his mind and give starters more minutes than he had planned to, or may dress a player at the last minute, so that you don't ever know for sure who will be on the court in crunch time. Therefore, I recommend not betting too big during the preseason.

4. YOUNG NBA TEAMS FIND IT HARD TO WIN ON THE ROAD

The NBA is full of talent, but during the regular season and, even more so, in the playoffs, experience makes the difference. Experienced teams are able to execute down the stretch both offensively and defensively, while young inexperienced teams crumble under the pressure and tend to take bad shots with the game on the line. Young teams also find ways to lose. Young teams tend to need the home crowd behind them to sustain their energy and confidence in order to close out games. When they are on the road, they do not have that support.

The NBA is a game of runs: Whoever has the best run in the fourth quarter will probably win the game, as long as the score was close going into the stretch. After 40 minutes, a young road team can build a 6-point lead, for example, but 6 points in an NBA game isn't much. A home team can come back in a matter of minutes to steal the game. In the NBA, 75 to 80 percent of games are in winnable range for both teams heading into the fourth quarter. The quick 24-second shot clock and scoring ability of the players are part of the reason that small leads heading into the fourth quarter often evaporate in minutes.

The Cleveland Cavaliers had a young team in 2003. It's hard to believe the record they had: Between January 13 and December 13, spanning two seasons, Cleveland lost 34 consecutive road games! Even after they drafted superstar Lebron James for the 2003-2004 season, the team had eight road losses before they finally ended the streak. They were a young and inexperienced team that could not close out games on the road. It was no surprise that after they traded away two of their young, talented players, Ricky Davis and Darius Miles, for quality, experienced role players Eric Williams, Tony Battie and point guard Jeff McInnis, Cleveland became a decent road team.

Young teams traditionally have terrible road records, while experienced teams finish with decent road records. I watched a game between the Orlando Magic on the road facing the Los Angeles Lakers in the 2003-2004 NBA season. The Lakers had a solid home record, while the Orlando Magic had one of the worst road records in the NBA. I tuned into the game with

11 minutes left in the fourth quarter. With Orlando up by 11 points, I made a friendly wager with my brother that the Lakers would win the game. The Lakers rallied and won the game in overtime. Orlando could not make plays down the stretch, taking some bad shots and committing careless turnovers. That's exactly what young teams do on the road—falter down the stretch.

If you find an opportunity to wager against unproven, young road teams, take advantage of it. When you bet on a road team, make sure you are betting on an experienced veteran road team that knows how to win games down the stretch.

5. HOW TO WAGER ON OVER/UNDERS IN THE NBA

Over/unders can be a profitable way to make money betting pro basketball. You want to analyze your bets based on these two factors:

A. THE TEMPO OF THE GAME

Is the game going to be fast-paced or slow-paced? You must analyze the teams' styles of play by watching them. You also should analyze the recaps and box scores of their most recent games and the entire season. You must be able to predict what kind of game it's going to be.

B. THE MATCHUPS

Are there serious mismatches? Is one team's size likely to dominate the other team's small frontcourt? Are the players on the court offensive or defensive players? Is one team's quickness going to run all over the other team's slow backcourt players? If there are mismatches, chances are good that the game is going to be higher scoring than the over/under spread for the game.

In betting over/unders, you can take advantage of trades, new coaches or new situations, while Vegas will often be making the spread based on the team's average for the season. The Chicago Bulls were one of the higher scoring teams in the league early in the 2003-2004 NBA Season. Then they made a blockbuster trade that brought in two defensive players and hired a defensive coach. Suddenly, their style of play became slower-paced as the players they put on the court were strong defensively but weak offensively. As a result, the Bulls' games started going under.

In betting over/unders, even more than in game spreads, timeliness in your bets is important. If you like a bet, take it right away, as the line can move 1 to 3 points, sometimes even 4 to 6 points, in the other direction.

The following is my recommendation when making over/under wagers.

- In an NBA game, if you want to wager the over, wager the whole game over.
- In an NBA game, if you want to wager the under, wager the first half under only.

Here are two reasons why I recommend when wagering over/unders to take first halves under and full games over.

A. OVERTIME

I recommend taking the first half under and the full game over when wagering over/unders because about 5 to 10 percent of NBA games end up in a tie after 48 minutes, thus getting an extra five minutes of playing time. Five minutes adds to the length of an NBA game by 10.42 percent. Chances are good that those five minutes will make or break your wager, unless it has already gone over. Why would you bet an under in a game that might have an extra five minutes to it? An extra five minutes of game time will almost always take an over bet over the top with the extra points, and crush what appeared to be a good under bet.

B. LATE GAME FREE THROWS

In many NBA games during the fourth quarter, teams have no better choice than intentionally fouling the opponent to stop the game clock from running out. This happens when between 0.1 seconds and one minute are left in the game, and usually when a team has a lead of 8 points or less, depending on the score and situation. About 9 points or more usually is the figure when most head coaches decide to wave the white flag and admit that the lead is too insurmountable to come back.

Imagine a scenario in which the Lakers are up by 4 points with 20 seconds left in a game when the Blazers score a layup to get within 2 points. The shot clock is only 24 seconds, so the Lakers could hold the ball the rest of the way. The Blazers foul the Lakers to prolong the game and just hope that the Lakers miss a free throw. The Lakers may hit both or only one free throw, and the Blazers look for a quick score the other way. This type of free-throw game with the clock ticking down can really rack up the points. Isiah Thomas once scored 15 points in the last 90 seconds of an NBA playoff game! During the 2004-2005 NBA season, Tracy McGrady scored an amazing 13 points in less than 40 seconds, because Houston kept fouling to stop the clock.

Many NBA games have a significant number of intentional fouls toward the end of the game—sometime as many as five.

This affects your wagers. An NBA game is 48 minutes long. In an average NBA minute, about 4 points total are scored. If you multiply 4 points by 48 minutes, you get 192 points, which is pretty close to the average score in an NBA game. But in the last minute of an NBA game, instead of four points being scored, up to 10 to 14 points can be scored. This adds an extra 6 to 10 points to the final total in a game. When you are betting the whole game over, this is great, because these points can often put your over bet over the top!

In the last minute of a game the total can be inflated so you are better off betting the under in the first half. Actually, during the last minute of the first half, teams often hold for one shot with 28 or fewer seconds left in the game when they get the possession, causing the score to be deflated in the last minute of a first half.

Late-game free throws are a key reason why I recommend betting unders only on first halves.

6. WHAT TO LOOK FOR IN NBA OVER/ UNDER BETS

With over/unders wagers, it is important to know a team's style of play, which often can be more important than its talent on paper. After 10 games or so into the season, you need to figure out what each NBA team is made of. Are they a run and gun team? Are they a good defensive half-court team? Are they a terrible passing team? Do they have good shooters? Do they have guys who go to the free throw line? Do they rebound the basketball well? Do they slow it down every time? Do they live and die by the jumper, or do they get a lot of lay-ups and dunks? You need to know all these things about every team. You have to watch games to see a team's style of play.

One of the most important factors determining whether a game will go over or under is a team's fast-break game. If a team consistently runs to get easy baskets, that team can be more reliable for an over wager. If a team strictly looks to score in the half court, they are less reliable for an over. Teams change their styles during the season, so keep a close eye on which teams are running and gunning and which are not. In the NBA a team can have a good offensive talent base on paper, but with a coach who loves to slow it down, the team won't score points. A team might also have good scorers, but no good passers, so its offense may not click.

NBA over/unders on any given day can go anywhere from 160 to 230 points or even higher, depending on who is playing. Don't be afraid to bet over on a line such as 204 or 205 if you find two great offenses with weak defenses playing against each other. Each year there are about seven or eight teams that are really good offensively and play poor defense. If two of the top eight high-scoring teams are playing each other, chances are good that the game will go over 204. Sometimes it can be good to bet under 190 if you find two struggling offenses, especially if a key offensive player out. However, never bet a first half under 85 points or less, because you are leaving yourself no room for error. If the teams get hot, you can easily lose, no matter who is playing. Don't bet too many low spreads under or too many high spreads over. You can find two efficient offenses with a spread of 186, if you look carefully.

To get an edge, you have to be able to classify all players as either "over" players or "under" players. An over player helps a game go over; an under player helps a game go under. In other words, an over player is more of an offensive player, while an under player is more of a defensive player.

Let's say that in 2005, you bet the Dallas Mavericks and Cleveland Cavaliers game to go over 185 points. There are two key players in the game: One can really help the game go over, while the other helps the game go under. Dirk Nowitzki is a pure "over" player. He is a great shooter and scorer, he easily hits threes, he goes to the foul line, and he can play great offense. But he can be a weak man-to-man defender, so that on the other side of the court, he is helping the game go over as well. Overall, the more minutes Nowitzki plays, the more he helps the game go over. I remember one game when Tim Duncan scored over 50 points while Nowitzki covered him.

On the other side of the court for Cleveland, there is Ben Wallace. Wallace, a multi-year Defensive Player of the Year award winner, is one of the biggest "under" players in the league. He blocks shots, changes shots, rebounds well (preventing easy offensive rebounding points), and plays great man-to man-defense. However, he has no real offensive moves and is a terrible free throw shooter. When Wallace is in the game, he can effectively help the game be low scoring.

You use this information to your advantage by being aware of trades and injuries of key players. When a team has one or two key big men injured, that team will be more prone to play a smaller lineup, which will lead to more scoring and less defense. Look to bet the over in these situations. Two players out can make a big difference. If a team trades away two big guys for some small players, the team probably will start scoring more points. And if a team has key small scorers out of the lineup, their games will be much more likely to be low scoring.

Follow the teams and review their box scores. Who is getting the minutes? Is he an under or an over player? Read the trends before or as they happen to get a jump on the spreads.

As mentioned earlier, a perfect situation occurred in the 2003-2004 season with the Chicago Bulls. The Bulls had one of the worst defenses in the NBA early on, but they had a great offense. They then traded two good offensive (over) players in Jalen Rose and Donyell Marshall to Toronto for two defensive (under) players, Jerome Williams and Antonio Davis. They actually put Jerome and Antonio in the starting lineup. Their offense fell apart, and it did not help that Eddy Curry, their key scoring forward, got injured. I bet one of their games under 90 in the first half against Detroit in December of 2003. The score at halftime was 35-25 for Detroit—I won the bet by 30 points! I bet a number of other Bulls games under for the next few weeks until the spread was adjusted, and I was extremely successful. On the other hand, the Toronto Raptors games went over the total consistently for the next few weeks, as they had two new quality scorers and still had low over/under spreads.

European players, for the most part, are great offensive players, but usually weak defenders and this is a good way to adjust for your bets. In general, the more European players who are getting minutes, the more likely it is that your game will go over. Dirk Nowitzki, Toni Kukoc, Peja Strokavic, Rik Smits, and Vladimir Radminovic were, or currently are, all great offensive players, but are weak on defense, or maybe average at best.

In betting over/unders in the NBA, the point guards are key. They create plays and dictate tempo with the fast break game; in other words, they run the show. They are like quarterbacks and can make a huge difference in whether you win or lose your over/under bet. If a key point guard for any NBA team will not be playing in a given game, and the team does not have a decent backup to pick up the slack, there's a good chance that his team will struggle to put points on the board. Chris Paul and Steve Nash are two perfect examples of point guards who control the offensive production of their teams.

Below is a list of NBA players and my classification of them as either over or under players.

NBA OVER/UNDER PLAYERS	
Dirk Nowitzki - Over	Ben Wallace - Under*
Lebron James - Over	Alonzo Mourning - Under
Dwayne Wade - Over	Bruce Bowen - Under
Steve Nash - Over*	Marcus Camby - Under
Chris Paul - Over	Greg Buckner - Under
Carmelo Anthony - Over	Michael Olawakandi - Under
Allen Iverson - Over*	DeSagana Diop - Under*
Baron Davis - Over	Eric Dampier - Under
* An extremely one-sided player	

Remember you are always looking for changes to take advantage of the spread—a change in coach, injuries, trades and players' playing time.

When betting over/unders in the NBA, follow this process:

1. Find a high or low spread that catches your eye and that you like.
2. Read the game preview to pick up any possible info.
3. Go to covers.com or any reputable injury-reporting site to look at the injury reports to see who is playing and who will not be playing.
4. Review the box scores and recaps of all the meetings between the two teams so far on the season to get a feel for what has happened previously.

5. See how both teams have fared in their last five to seven games. How many points are they scoring and giving up per game?

6. Check the box scores of the last five to seven games that each team has played to see which players are getting the minutes. If smaller, more skilled players are getting a lot more minutes, the over may be a good bet, and vice versa.

7. Make your decision. Do you like a bet? How much do you like it? How many units will you bet?

7. COLLEGE BASKETBALL TIPS AND STRATEGIES

College basketball is a sport with ample handicapping opportunities. The great thing about college basketball is that there are many games to choose from. Between November and March, there can be 10 to 70 or more games every day. The more games or lines you have to choose from, the better chance you have of finding a bet that is good or great. Keep a keen eye on the top 25 teams and follow them during the season. Then put your time in to learn about the other teams.

Following are a few key tips and strategies that you can use to your success.

TIPS

1. BE VERY PICKY
Only bet on the games that you are very confident in.

2. KNOW YOUR SPORT
Follow teams in the top 25 as well as other teams. You may be able to get an inside scoop on a local team. Follow injuries and the teams' progress.

3. WATCH AS MUCH COLLEGE BASKETBALL AS POSSIBLE
Watching games allows you to see how a team really plays, not just what the box scores on the Internet tell you. Keep track of a team's strengths and weaknesses as well as its pace of play. A team's pace of play is the most important thing in making money in over/unders in college basketball. Box scores and re-caps are good, but there is nothing better than watching teams play!

4. REMEMBER THAT TEAMS GET NEW PLAYERS EVERY YEAR
Seniors graduate and new freshmen come in to play, so don't just bet on the name of the team. Make sure the team has good players. If you find that a team is overrated, bet against it early in the season if the talent is weak.

5. HOME COURT ADVANTAGE
Don't get tempted into betting on road teams with good spreads. If you bet on a road team, bet on a *proven* road team playing against a team that is on a much lesser level in terms of talent. Home court advantage is so huge that some teams play great at home and play terrible on the road. Find out who these teams are and make money when the right opportunity comes along.

In postseason and preseason NCAA tournaments, two teams face each other on a so-called neutral court. However, some of these neutral courts give one team the home court advantage. If a game is played within a reasonable drive to the school's campus (one to four hours), hoards of fans often will make the drive to the game and create a home court advantage. For example, in the NCAA tournament Butler once played Tennessee in Alabama. You wouldn't think that either team had the home court advantage, but the Tennessee campus was only three hours from the game location. Thousands of fans made the drive to watch the game and gave Tennessee added support to help them to victory. Find out for sure if the distance from the team's campus to where the game is being played is close. This way you will really know if you are wagering on a game with a neutral court or a home court advantage.

6. DON'T BE COMFORTABLE BETTING A 2 TO 5 POINT DOG

At times, 2 to 5 point dogs can be good bets, but be careful because college teams will foul right down to the last second if the game is in any kind of reach. Fouling often allows a favorite with a 2-point lead and 30 seconds left to win the game by 6 to 8 points. If you bet on a team at +2 to 5 points, you have to believe that they have a solid chance of winning the game outright. If you don't think they can win the game outright, then 2 to 5 points with a spread is no good—you should be looking for 7 or 8 points.

7. BET WHAT YOU KNOW!

Don't bet big money on a game unless you are sure you know what you are doing.

STRATEGIES

1. BET ON HOT TEAMS, BET AGAINST COLD TEAMS

A simple but always effective strategy, especially with young players, is to bet on hot teams and against cold teams, as confidence is a definite factor.

2. BET ON HOME TEAMS

You often can find equally or better talented teams playing at home with a very low spread. Consider betting on them. You may see that one team is 8-1 at home while their opponent is 4-5 on the road. Both have played a similar caliber of opponents, yet the spread is 2 to 4 points. Bet with good home teams and you can have an edge.

3. BET AGAINST INJURED TEAMS

Teams with injured star players often cannot make up for their absence because the star is just too good. In the NBA, there may be a great veteran backup, but in college there usually is not anyone ready to match the injured star player's production. If you think that a team will really struggle with their key player out, look to bet against them.

4. OVER/UNDER TIP

The over and under in a college basketball game is usually 10 points higher in the second half than the first half. A standard line of 130 will usually consist of 60 for the first half and 70 for the second half.

Sometimes you can find really good wagers by betting the first half over. If you check out the spreads on a daily basis, you can find some low first-half spreads in the 50 to 60 range. Find two teams that have shown consistent ability to put the ball in the basket and score, focusing on their last five to seven games. Look to bet the over if you get a line in the 50s because there is room for error.

If you bet the right game over 55 for the first half, there is a realistic window that the game will be 50 to 73 points. You will often be in position to win. Don't get tempted to bet really low first halves over that are at 53 or less, because often these games come in low.

Over/under results in college basketball often come down to tempo. For the most part, two up-tempo teams will do a lot of scoring; one up-tempo team and one low-scoring team can balance out to an average scoring game; and two low-tempo teams will lead to low scoring. If you can find a low spread with two up-tempo teams, or a high spread with two low-tempo teams, you could have a good bet.

During the college basketball season, take a look at the daily NCAA over/under spreads and analyze the following main factors:

Read the game preview to get a good feel for the game. In the preview you may possibly get a few tidbits of information that can help.

Check the game's final scores for each team, focusing on the past five games. Have they been scoring lately, or are they cold? Who is getting the minutes in their last few games? Big guys or small guys?

Did the teams play each other earlier in the season? If so, analyze not only the box score, read the game recap. The recap may tell you that both teams were really hot or really cold in that particular game. Chances are good that hot or cold shooting will not occur again, so you may get an edge since the spread is partially based on that first game. If the two teams have not played yet during the year, check to see if they played last year and note what happened. However, only look at last year's game as a factor if the rosters and key players on both sides are similar to the current team.

Check for injuries. If one or two key scorers are out, their absence can definitely sway you from taking the over to possibly taking the under.

Narrow your selections and then only take the best ones, if any at all.

If you are selective and follow college basketball closely, you can find teams that are equal in talent at +7 to 10 points either at home or on a neutral court. This may occur due to a bias in a Vegas spread, a slump, or that a team has been underachieving. The bottom line is that, if you can have 7 to 10 points in your pocket with five college players playing five other college players, there's no reason why your underdog cannot win or, at the least, cover the spread.

College basketball is a good sport to bet on because you are able to choose the games you bet on from the hundreds of choices every week. Use the tips and strategies listed above and, if you do your homework, you can be successful wagering on the right college basketball games.

CHAPTER
16

4 TOP TIPS FOR BETTING OTHER SPORTS

1. DIVERSIFY YOUR SPORTS KNOWLEDGE TO CAPITALIZE ON MORE OPPORTUNITIES

Most sports books these days offer wagering on many different sports besides the main four team sports. Tennis, boxing, soccer, golf, motor racing, the WNBA, Olympic events and proposition life/society bets are just a sampling of available bets.

A lot of people like betting on soccer. I don't bet soccer because if two evenly matched teams are playing each other, your bet is dependent on whether or not the ball goes into the net in one or two big plays in the game. As I've stated earlier, I don't like putting big money on matches that are decided by one or two plays.

Boxing can be a good sport to bet on because it is just one man versus another man. However, be careful because fights can be decided by judges who are either biased or wrong in their decisions. In boxing, the line set up by Vegas and the sports books can often be linked more to the boxer's popularity than to the boxer's current fighting ability. Vegas will set the line on the match so that sports books end up accepting equal wagering and balance their books; they don't set the line based on a true current boxing value of each fighter. The popular fighter may be at -120 when it really should be his opponent, the better fighter, at -225. This gives you good betting opportunities.

Look to bet against boxers who generate a lot of hype. For example, in June, 2005, Mike Tyson was a big favorite against Kevin McBride, a no-name boxer. McBride was about a 7 to 1 underdog to win. Tyson's career was winding down, if not already finished. Tyson was dominated in the fifth and sixth rounds and lost in a sixth round TKO. The line was based on public perception, not the true odds of who would win. Tyson probably should have been a small favorite, not a big one.

If there is a sport that you specialize in (besides the four major team sports), you can gain a betting advantage over the sports books if you know a lot more than the average bettor.

2. HOCKEY WAGERING

Of the four major sports, I have found that hockey is by far the hardest to wager on, because there is so much parity. You can analyze a game all you want, but a hot goalie can beat you, or an underdog can squeak out a 2 to 1 win, and still no one is screaming upset. The home ice advantage is not as big as it is in basketball and football. But a good basic strategy for hockey betting is really simple: Bet on hot teams and against cold teams.

One good thing about betting hockey is that even if a team has won five of its last six games in a row, you can often still get a good money line! Be careful betting against hot goalies, because a goalie can single-handedly win games or playoff series. You often will find a team being outshot 39 to 25 and outplayed by the other team for the whole game, and yet they still win the game 3 to 2. How frustrating is that!

Goalies often go on hot and cold streaks. When they're hot, they stop every puck they see—the only ones they don't stop are the ones that are screened or the puck gets deflected. Over the years, many goalies have helped teams win games or series that they had no right winning. In the 2003 NHL playoffs, for example, Jean-Sebastien Giguere of Anaheim carried the Ducks to the NHL finals. The Ducks had almost no right beating Detroit in the first round of the playoffs, but Giguere made more than 60 saves multiple times to help win that series.

You can also bet against teams that have a major case of the injury bug.

If I find the right matchup, I'll take a hockey team to beat the other team in a seven game series. I know that one play will not beat me, but a series of games can make me a winner or loser at the end. But beware: The NHL playoffs over the years have been loaded with upsets, with 8-seeds beating 1-seeds, and 7-seeds beating 2-seeds.

3. TENNIS WAGERING

Tennis is a sport of human versus human combat on a neutral court. There are few variables, and every play is worth the same: 1 point. For an upset to happen, the underdog simply must outplay the favorite. If you believe that the underdog has little chance of beating the favorite, bet on the favorite in confidence. Keep in mind, however, that underdogs win quite often in tennis.

Lines of -150 to -400 can be good wagers. When betting on underdogs in tennis, see if you can get a very good money line of +300 or higher when you think that your player has a legitimate shot of winning. I once wagered on a women's underdog in Wimbledon who won one of her matches at 18 to 1 odds!

Bet good money on your favorites when you have a lot of confidence that they will win. Bet small on underdogs that you think have a shot. If you know tennis, you can make money in this sport. Here are four keys to success in wagering on tennis:

A) BET ON HOT PLAYERS AND AGAINST COLD PLAYERS

Form is by far the most important factor when betting on tennis. Players who have won nine of their last twelve matches are hot and on their game, while players who have only won two of their last twelve matches are cold and are off their game. Motivation, performance and consistency are easy to detect by reviewing a player's recent results.

Check how these players have fared in recent tournaments, or how they are playing in their current tournament. Have they lost their last five matches or have they won their last three matches? Are they dominating their competition in straight sets, or are they squeaking by in the deciding set? A player is more likely to lose in a tournament if he or she has struggled to advance in the prior match. A player who is cruising by is more likely to win his following match in the same tournament.

Tennis is all about players being on the top of their game. Hot players find a way to make shots; cold players miss shots. A hot or cold player is so significant in tennis, that it should be the main factor in placing your wager.

B) BET ON PLAYERS WHO ARE PLAYING ON THEIR BEST SURFACE, AND AGAINST ONES PLAYING ON THEIR WORST SURFACE

The main tennis surfaces are hardcourt, grass and clay. However, some of the best tennis players in the world cannot play on clay, which is favorable to short, quick players with good ground strokes. Most of the Latin players are excellent competing on clay. Grass is favorable to tall players with big serves and a good volley game, because the ball stays low on that surface. For example, Wimbledon was a good surface for big servers such as Pete Sampras. Hardcourt is the most popular surface, and most players are comfortable playing on it.

As great a player as he was, Pete Sampras never won the French Open. Why? It's a clay surface, which is good for fast players because the surface slows down big serves. On clay you have to able to slide around the court to get to the ball. Most players on tour cannot slide that effectively. Players such as Guillermo Coria were amazing on clay; he was one of the top two players in the world on that surface for some time. However, Coria would have had problems beating a 50th ranked player on grass, whereas Andy Roddick is average on clay and dominant on grass.

If you want to be successful wagering on tennis, you must be able to determine who plays well on which surfaces. When breaking down wagers that you like, find each player's recent (one to two years) record on the surface he will be playing on.

Surface is the second most important factor to a players form in analyzing tennis wagers.

C) BET ON PLAYERS WHO HAVE A GOOD HEAD-TO-HEAD RECORD AGAINST THEIR OPPONENT

If a player has a winning record head-to-head against his or her opponent, there is a significant chance that the next time they play together, he or she will beat that opponent again. If one player beat another player 6-2, 6-2 two months ago, it is a good indication that that player will beat the same opponent in their next meeting. However, if the final score was 6-7, 7-6, 7-5, there's a good chance that both players are evenly matched.

Another factor in head-to-head results is matchups. Some types of players match up very well against certain other types of players. Quick players usually match up well against big servers on clay courts, while big servers can dominate short, quick players on grass courts. Style of play is very important when looking at matchups between two players. You can find tennis head-to-head info on the Internet at the main sites of the ATP, which is atptennis.com, and the WTA, which is sonyericsson-wtatour.com.

If you can get an underdog that is anywhere from 2 to 1 to 8 to 1 odds in a match, and he or she has already beaten that opponent once out of three previous matches, you might have a good underdog wager. If it was done once, it can be done again. Sometimes there is not much of a talent difference between a 7th ranked player and a 30th ranked player. If a 30th ranked player just makes a few more plays and a few less mistakes, he or she can easily be victorious. The 18 to 1 bet that I won in Wimbledon was Eleni Daniilidou over Justine Henin-Hardenne. Daniilidou had won one and lost one head-to-head versus Hardenne going in. I was not confident that Eleni would win, but at 18 to 1, it was a good bet.

D) BET AGAINST INJURED OR RUSTY PLAYERS

Some players will participate in a big tournament even though they are hampered by injury. Injured players, not surprisingly, often get upset early in these tournaments. In 2005, in the French Open, Andre Agassi was upset in the first round by Jarkko Nieminen. Agassi was suffering through a terrible nerve problem in his back and ended up losing in five sets, barely able to finish the match. Look for injuries in betting tennis.

Look to bet against players who are coming back after taking a significant layoff if you like the match and can get the right points. These players are often rusty and their injuries could still be nagging. It takes time, usually weeks if not months and at least three to five matches or more for a player to come back from an injury to 100 percent of his or her playing form. Reading the recaps of certain matches, you will notice that players often tip their own hand by admitting that they are playing in a lot of pain and think they will have a tough time winning their next match.

The main tennis websites of the ATP and WTA will give you everything you need to know about a certain player, including age, season record history, favorite surface, how he/she has done in head-to-head previous matches versus different opponents, and anything else you need.

Remember that underdogs come through and win quite often. One key tip is that underdogs sometimes beat big favorites when the favorite is tired and is coming off a long week in a previous tournament where he or she made the finals. These players often will lose because they are not hungry for the win or need some time off. Minor tournaments go from Monday to Sunday, while major tournaments run from Monday through two Sundays. Some players have different priorities and like to focus on certain tournaments or playing surfaces. Consider all these factor when betting tennis.

Also consider home court advantage, which can be a factor if a player is competing in his or her home country. Players really want to be at their best when they are playing at home, and often step up their game in these situations.

However, look for weak or terrible players who squeak into a tournament as a wildcard entry. They are playing in their home country and the tournament directors want local players participating so that the crowds will show up to cheer them on. These players can be quite overmatched, making their opponents a great wager to win.

In men's tennis, in a best-of-five match, the player favored to win has a stronger chance of winning compared to a best-of-three match. The underdog is more likely to upset in a shorter, best-of-three match. The Grand Slam and Davis Cup matches are best-of-five sets for men, while all other men's tournaments are best-of-three sets. All women's WTA tennis matches are best-of-three sets.

The best and simplest advice I can give for tennis wagering is this: Find wagers where you are betting on great players against weak players at low money lines. A major disparity in talent between two players is what you are always looking for. You usually can find these wagers in the first or second rounds of most tournaments.

4. INTERNATIONAL EVENTS

"Why should I wager on international events when I can just wager on domestic events like the NBA, the NFL and major league baseball?" you might wonder. First and foremost, the linesmakers often do not know where to set a line in these international events, so you may be able to find spreads that are off base. Secondly, in the four major domestic sports these days, there is a great deal of parity, whereas in international sporting events, there is a wide range in the talent levels between teams and players. Therefore, you are able to take advantage of one of the best strategies in sports gambling—betting on strength and against weakness.

In a FIBA basketball game, one team often is favored by 25 points. And in a hockey game, one team may be favored by 5 1/2 goals. When you find an international event with a big spread, do research to see if there is any advantage in betting the underdog. You also may end up seeing that the favorite is a good wager. In an NBA game, I rarely take a team -13 points, but in an international game, I will take a team -18 points if they have consistently beaten teams by 20, 30 or 40 points.

I have seen spreads in international events that have been way off. I have seen a 16-point favorite lose the game outright and a 20-point underdog win outright. I have also seen some teams destroy their opponents in a soccer game 8 to 0 and a basketball team destroy their opponent by 60 points. I once made money on a FIBA juniors basketball game between two different countries, in which one team was favored by 15 points. After doing my research, I determined that the underdog had much more talent and the spread was off by at least 25 points. Actually, the underdog team should have been favored by at least 10 points!

My underdog ended up winning the game by 17 points. I made money with the spread and the money line in that game.

When you find an international event with a great underdog at plus big points, balance it out and make two wagers. Put more money on the spread and less on the money line. If you at least cover the spread, you are still up; and if you win the game outright, you win big money on the money line and the spread.

The spread in international events may be off because it can be based on previous years' head-to-head results, not on the actual talent of the current roster. For example, I once wagered on Turkey in Euro League basketball at +9 points against Lithuania in the first game of a major tournament. Lithuania had a history of excellence in international basketball, but they did not send a talented team to the games that year, while Turkey was playing very well heading into the tournament. The spread was partially based on Lithuania's greatness in international basketball and the fact that they had won this tournament four years earlier. Turkey ended up winning the game outright by a few points.

Talent is the most important factor in any sporting event. Therefore, if you can bet against a team when the spread is too high because their talent is overrated (based on tradition or other factors), you are in a good position to win.

The question is, "How do you find good and great wagers in international sporting events?" Here is a simple step-by-step process that you can use:

1) LOGIC

In any wager, you need to understand the dynamics of the sport. Do not wager on a sporting event that you know little about and don't know the players involved. If you know nothing about cricket, don't bet on cricket. Use common sense: If you like betting on college and pro basketball—and know these sports—look for opportunities with FIBA and Olympic basketball events. Bet the sport that you know best.

2) RESEARCH

How your team or player has performed recently is of utmost importance. Don't look back at, say, the previous Olympics as a guide to your wagers in the current Olympics. Four years is a lot of time, teams change, players get older, new athletes step up to the international stage. For example, if you are betting on world championship basketball, you should check out each team's pre-tournament games to see how they fared. Comparing head-to-head results between similar opponents is the main barometer to use for international events. Review the results of at least three games, not just one. Anyone or any team can have one great game or one terrible game.

Always do thorough research on the Internet. Let's say that you want to research the pre-Olympic results of the Australian men's basketball team. Just go to Google and enter "Australia men's basketball," and browse as many entries as you have to until you can find the team's most recent results.

Each international competition you wager on should have its own website. These sites should have recent results and a complete roster list for each team. I often compare that roster list to the box scores of other games to determine whether the same players are playing that played three months ago in an exhibition game. If the same players are playing, it can be a good barometer; if they are not, the info can be misleading. For example, the Argentina basketball team changes for each tournament. Sometimes they get all their NBA players to compete. Other times they get only a few of them to participate, depending on which event it is and who is healthy or available at the time.

3) GEOGRAPHICAL ADVANTAGE

Be aware of possible home court advantages. For example, if you are betting against the New Zealand basketball team and the game is being played in Australia, there is a good chance that New Zealand will have a lot of fans making the trip to the game, especially if it's a big event. Or if you are betting against Spain and the game is being played in Madrid, be careful because their home court advantage will be huge. In international competitions, home advantage is big in team sports. However, it is not much of a factor in individual sports such as skiing or track.

For the most part, wagers that you make in international events involve two teams facing each other on a neutral playing field. Often, you can find opportunities where the favorite should not be favored quite as heavily.

4) POOR SPREADS

International events offer many opportunities to take advantage of poor spreads. If a spread catches your eye, research the game. The spread may be accurate, but with international events, spreads are frequently way off base. Take advantage of these opportunities when you find them.

5) WATCH TEAMS AND PLAYERS PERFORM

If you are betting on Olympic basketball, hockey, or any other international wager, watch your team or player perform if you can. There is no substitute for this. By watching them, you can determine whether you have enough reasons and trust to wager on them. Regardless of spread, sometimes you can watch one team and be very impressed, while at the same time, you can watch another team and be very disappointed as you see them making stupid mistakes.

I once wagered on a basketball team based purely on stats because I hadn't had a chance to watch them play. Luckily, I ended up winning my wager. However, after getting a chance to watch them play, I knew that I would never bet on them again. Why? Because, even though they had good talent, they played poorly as a team.

CHAPTER 17

WRAPPING IT UP

To ensure long term profit, you have to make only good or great wagers, and you have to bet bigger money on the best wagers you find.

"What is a great wager you ask?" There are several things you can look for. One of them is when a spread is off base and you can take advantage of it. Another great bet is when you can find a major disparity in the talent levels of two teams and a low spread to go with it. When you just know that one team is going to destroy the other team, and you have that low spread, that's a great bet. There is nothing better in sports gambling then this! Another hallmark of a great bet is one in which you feel confident you can destroy the spread or at least beat it easily, giving you the confidence to put solid money down on those wagers.

Your goal is to show a net profit after every year. To be successful, you need to put in the adequate amount of time needed to research and analyze the spreads—at least one to two hours a day during the peak sports betting season.

If there is a wager you like, take as much time as you need to analyze and research it before deciding if and how much you want to wager on it. Try not to overanalyze a game; either something stands out right from the outset or it does not.

Knowledge is power, so it is vital that you watch an adequate number of games and make smart wagers. You will experience bad days, but your goal is to win the marathon, not a few sprints.

The two most important things you control over the sports books and Vegas are:

1. What you bet on.
2. How much you bet on it.

Why is this so key? It is because you have to be selective in your wagers, and you have to know when to bet big. Even if for five days straight you find no good bets and make no wagers, therefore making no money, well, at least being even is better than losing money. In the long term, you are not going to be profitable betting big money on matches that in your head you know can go either way. You may win on any one day, but the only way to win long term is to make every wager a good or great wager, not a toss-up wager.

When you are looking to make a bet, two simple thoughts will often help you determine if and how much you bet on it: "I think I will win this bet," or "I know I should win this bet." Skip the bet when the first condition applies—or at least, bet the minimum—and when the second condition applies, make a solid wager within the money management guidelines we covered earlier.

Information is a key to making money! But current information is what you should be looking for, not useless info like, hypothetically, the 49ers are 12-3 lifetime against Miami. Remember that you are betting on the present team and players on that team, and should use recent information on how these teams have been playing. Also look for injuries, which do influence outcomes.

Here's another invaluable tip: Control your emotions! I cannot emphasize this enough. Don't get too high or too low! Don't believe in being hot or cold, believe in finding good and great wagers. If you get on a good streak don't consider yourself to be hot, consider yourself to be fortunate that you found a lot of good and great wagers and took advantage of them. Thinking like that keeps you making good bets.

Always bet in a controlled manner, keeping with the 1 to 4 unit bet range. If you have lost a few key wagers, do not force a big bet on a "lock" just to get even. There are no locks and one big bet can dig you deeper into a hole. The best piece of advice I can give you if you're on a losing streak: Slow down and become more selective in your bets.

Never go into a week or month and think that you want to make x number of bets, or win x amount of money. And never bet big because you want to buy extra presents for the holiday season, you want to buy an expensive gift for your sister's birthday, or you're just looking for action. Only bet big when you find great bets. Be patient and they will come. You'll make money by finding great wagers one at a time! Just look to take advantage of every favorable wager that you can find, be it one bet a week or five bets a week. There are some weeks where you may find only one or two good bets to make; if so, that is all you should make. The fewer bets you make the easier it should be to win, because that means you are being selective and only taking the best wagers.

It is up to you to succeed as a sports gambler; the more you know about sports and about the quality of different teams and players, the more opportunities you will have. If you don't follow a certain sports league at all, don't try and make money in it. You have to know how different games flow to get profitable wagers.

I hope that you have become a better sports handicapper with the information in this book. These strategies work for me and I am confident that they can work for you as well. I wish you all the success in your journey as a sports gambler. Remember, luck will balance out over the long haul and success will only come by following the sports you bet on, managing your money, and by finding and betting sensibly on good and great wagers!

POWERFUL WINNING POKER SIMULATIONS
A MUST FOR SERIOUS PLAYERS WITH A COMPUTER!
IBM compatible CD ROM Win 95, 98, 2000, NT, ME, XP

These incredible full color poker simulations are the best method to improve your game. Computer opponents play like real players. All games let you set the limits and rake and have fully programmable players, plus stat tracking, and Hand Analyzer for starting hands. MIke Caro, the world's foremost poker theoretician says, "Amazing... a steal for under $500... get it, it's great." Includes free phone support. "Smart Advisor" gives expert advice for every play!

1. TURBO TEXAS HOLD'EM FOR WINDOWS - $59.95. Choose which players, and how many (2-10) you want to play, create loose/tight games, and control check-raising, bluffing, position, sensitivity to pot odds, and more! Also, instant replay, pop-up odds, Professional Advisor keeps track of play statistics. Free bonus: Hold'em Hand Analyzer analyzes all 169 pocket hands in detail and their win rates under any conditions you set. Caro says this "hold'em software is the most powerful ever created." Great product!

2. TURBO SEVEN-CARD STUD FOR WINDOWS - $59.95. Create any conditions of play; choose number of players (2-8), bet amounts, fixed or spread limit, bring-in method, tight/loose conditions, position, reaction to board, number of dead cards, and stack deck to create special conditions. Features instant replay. Terrific stat reporting includes analysis of starting cards, 3-D bar charts, and graphs. Play interactively and run high speed simulation to test strategies. Hand Analyzer analyzes starting hands in detail. Wow!

3. TURBO OMAHA HIGH-LOW SPLIT FOR WINDOWS - $59.95. Specify any playing conditions; betting limits, number of raises, blind structures, button position, aggressiveness/passiveness of opponents, number of players (2-10), types of hands dealt, blinds, position, board reaction, and specify flop, turn, and river cards! Choose opponents and use provided point count or create your own. Statistical reporting, instant replay, pop-up odds high speed simulation to test strategies, amazing Hand Analyzer, and much more!

4. TURBO OMAHA HIGH FOR WINDOWS - $59.95. Same features as above, but tailored for Omaha High only. Caro says program is "an electrifying research tool...it can clearly be worth thousands of dollars to any serious player. A must for Omaha High players.

5. TURBO 7 STUD 8 OR BETTER - $59.95. Brand new with all the features you expect from the Wilson Turbo products: the latest artificial intelligence, instant advice and exact odds, play versus 2-7 opponents, enhanced data charts that can be exported or printed, the ability to fold out of turn and immediately go to the next hand, ability to peek at opponents hand, optional warning mode that warns you if a play disagrees with the advisor, and automatic mode that runs up to 50 tests unattended. Tough computer players vary their styles for a great game.

---

6. TOURNAMENT TEXAS HOLD'EM - $39.95

Set-up for tournament practice and play, this realistic simulation pits you against celebrity look-alikes. Tons of options let you control tournament size with 10 to 300 entrants, select limits, ante, rake, blind structures, freezeouts, number of rebuys and competition level of opponents. Pop-up status report shows how you're doing vs. the competition. Save tournaments in progress to play again later. Additional feature allows quick folds on finished hands.

DOYLE BRUNSON'S EXCITING BOOKS
ADD THESE TO YOUR COLLECTION - ORDER NOW!

SUPER SYSTEM *by Doyle Brunson.* This classic book is considered by the pros to be the best book ever written on poker! Jam-packed with advanced strategies, theories, tactics and money-making techniques, no serious poker player can afford to be without this hard-hitting information. Includes fifty pages of the most precise poker statistics ever published. Features chapters written by poker's biggest superstars, such as Dave Sklansky, Mike Caro, Chip Reese, Joey Hawthorne, Bobby Baldwin, and Doyle. Essential strategies, advanced play, and no-nonsense winning advice on making money at 7-card stud (razz, high-low split, cards speak, and declare); draw poker, lowball, and hold'em (limit and no-limit).This is a must-read for any serious poker player. 628 pages, $29.95.

SUPER SYSTEM 2 *by Doyle Brunson.* SS2 expands upon the original with more games and professional secrets from the best in the world. New revision includes Phil Hellmuth Jr. along with superstar contributors Daniel Negreanu, winner of multiple WSOP gold brace-lets and 2004 Poker Player of the Year; Lyle Berman, 3-time WSOP gold bracelet winner, founder of the World Poker Tour, and super-high stakes cash player; Bobby Baldwin, 1978 World Champion; Johnny Chan, 2-time World Champion and 10-time WSOP bracelet win-ner; Mike Caro, poker's greatest researcher, theorist, and instructor; Jennifer Harman, the world's top female player and one of ten best overall; Todd Brunson, winner of more than 20 tournaments; and Crandell Addington, no-limit hold'em legend. 704 pgs, $29.95.

CARO'S GUIDE TO DOYLE BRUNSON'S SUPER SYSTEM *by Mike Caro.* Working with World Champion Doyle Brunson, the legendary Mike Caro has created a fresh look to the "Bible" of all poker books, adding new and personal insights that help you understand the original work. Caro breaks 36 concepts into either "Analysis, Commentary, Concept, Mission, Play-By-Play, Psychology, Statistics, Story, or Strategy. Lots of illustrations and winning concepts give even more value to this great work. 86 pages, 8 1/2 x 11, $19.95.

ACCORDING TO DOYLE *by Doyle Brunson.* Learn what it takes to be a great poker player by climbing inside the mind of poker's most famous champion. Fascinating anecdotes and adventures from Doyle's early career playing poker in roadhouses are interspersed with lessons from the champion who has made more money at poker than anyone else in history. Learn what makes a great player tick, how he approaches the game, and receive candid, powerful advice from the legend himself. 208 pages, $14.95.

MY 50 MOST MEMORABLE HANDS *by Doyle Brunson.* This instant classic relives the most incredible hands by the greatest poker player of all time. Great players, legends, and poker's most momentous events march in and out of fifty years of unforgettable hands. Sit side-by-side with Doyle as he replays the excitement and life-changing moments of the most thrilling and crucial hands in the history of poker: from his early games as a rounder in the rough-and-tumble "Wild West" years—where a man was more likely to get shot as he was to get a straight flush—to the nail-biting excitement of his two world championship titles. Relive million dollar hands and the high stakes tension of sidestepping police, hijackers and murderers. A thrilling collection of stories and sage poker advice. 168 pages, $14.95.

THE GODFATHER OF POKER *by Doyle Brunson.* Doyle Brunson's riveting autobiography is a story of guts and glory, of good luck and bad, of triumph and unspeakable tragedy. It is a story of beating the odds, of a man who bet $1 million on a hole of golf—when he could barely stand! A master of the bluff, here is a man whose most outrageous bluff came with a gunman pointing a pistol at his forehead. He has survived whippings, gun fights, stabbings, mobsters, killers and a bout with cancer where the doctor told him his hand was played out. Apparently, fate had never played poker with Brunson; he lived. Doyle has searched for Noah's ark, tried to raise the Titanic, and won two poker championships. A must read. 352 pages, $26.95

BOOKS & ADVANCED STRATEGIES

BEAT THE SPORTS BOOKS: An Insider's Guide to Betting the NFL *Dan Gordon*. Living legend, Dan Gordon, a professional sports bettor and one of the world's best football handicappers, shares his inside tips and strategies on making consistent money betting on NFL football. Much of the information here—covering basic, advanced and expert concepts—is available nowhere else. Gordon's advice is brutally honest—and profitable. He shows how the *real* lines are set, how to establish your own betting lines and power ratings, how to separate performance from perception, how to beat point spreads, and money lines, bet underdogs, propositions, parlays, futures, and much more. 320 pages, **$19.95**.

SECRETS OF PROFESSIONAL SPORTS BETTING *by Michael Kochan*. This powerful manual is filled with 88 advanced sections that show you how to separate the truths and the myths of sports gambling and make money in the *real* world with *practical* strategies. The major sports are covered with a special emphasis on football and basketball, along with concepts, tips, theories and techniques that apply to all sports. In addition to hard-hitting specific strategies for recognizing opportunities and finding value—money line wagering, buying points, hedging bets, trends versus systems, incomplete rosters, travel schedules, over/under plays, prop bets, connected wagers, betting games (and *not* spreads)—Kochan includes keeping records, money management, analyzing wagers from both sides and how to think differently from the average loser. 256 pages, **$19.95**.

YOU CAN BET ON IT! *by Larry Grossman*. This revised edition brings together the top professionals in sports betting, legends such as Sonny Reizner and Lem Banker, men who actually set the betting lines. You'll learn how to bet and win at the major sports: football, baseball, basketball and prize fight betting. This easy-to-read and fact-filled book contains a wealth of information about how to read the lines, how the lines are made, the odds faced, handicapping, common mistakes, and other essentials. It features winning advice from the greatest pros in sports betting today. 224 pages, **$14.95**.

WINNING FANTASY FOOTBALL *by Stephen Nover*. One of America's foremost fantasy football experts shows *everything* you need to know to play and win at fantasy football. From the basic rules of play—how to score points, draft players, and join existing leagues or start your own—to the insider strategies and the essential fundamentals of building a winning team, you'll learn what it takes to be a winner. Learn when to draft star players, how to get value deep in the rounds, the tricks to finding sleepers and avoiding busts, how to improve your team through trades, pickups, and the waiver wire, the 10 basics of fantasy football, head-to-head, Rotisserie, salary cap, and keeper leagues, and draft & auction strategies. 276 pages, **$14.95**.

THE BASICS OF WINNING SPORTS BETTING *by Avery Cardoza*. This excellent primer shows you how to bet and win at football, baseball, basketball and boxing in one easy reading. You'll learn how to read the lines, how they're made, the odds, how the over/under, teasers and parlays work, more. 64 pages, **$4.95**.

DAN GORDON'S NFL HANDICAPPING (software) *by Dan Gordon*
A CD companion to *Beat the Sports Books*, this powerful program helps you handicap and win money at football betting. This includes identifying phony wins, phony losses, sloppy wins, home advantage adjustments and mid-season team rankings. It automatically calculates number power rankings, letter power rankings, due ups/downs, projected lines and win percentages and makes weekly adjustments according to Dan Gordon's 13 rules. You also get weekly updates to scores and handicapping data to Gordon's information via the Internet. **$90**.

WINNING FOOTBALL BETTOR: Van Paul's High-Tech New Winning Strategy
BEAT THE SPREAD: Augment solid handicapping skills with this winning strategy that shows how to analyze weather conditions for the extra edge to beat the bookie! Analyzes key positions and trends. The 5-Tier Safeguard Play debunks the "lock" fallacy and shows why to use your own strategies. Never buy tout sheets again. **Get the Hidden Edge!** Point by point, learn how types of teams react home/away under varying conditions - wind, heat, rain, mud and grime, snow, extreme cold, humidity, fog, "dome weather," — and how to bet "off-field" conditions, finesse, and how to win games that seem balanced to others, but actually give you an edge! Get a **$10 BONUS!** Van Paul's Underdog Best Play Pick's. **$50** Now Only **$25**.